Gender
Perspectives

Gender

ESSAYS ON WOMEN IN MUSEUMS

Perspectives

EDITED BY JANE R. GLASER
AND ARTEMIS A. ZENETOU

SMITHSONIAN INSTITUTION PRESS

Washington and London

Editor: Jenelle Walthour
Designer: Kathleen Sims

Library of Congress Cataloging-in-Publication Data
Gender perspectives : essays on women in museums / edited by Jane R.
    Glaser and Artemis A. Zenetou.
        p.   cm.
    Includes bibliographical references.
    ISBN 1-56098-325-6
    1. Museums—United States—Educational aspects. 2. Museums—
    United States—Management. 3. Women museum curators—United
    States. 4. Women in the professions—United States. 5. Sex role—
    United States. I. Glaser, Jane R. II. Zenetou, Artemis A.
    AM11.G45 1994
    069'.0973—dc20   93-19713

British Library Cataloguing-in-Publication Data is available

Manufactured in the United States of America
01 00 99 98 97 96 95 94   5 4 3 2 1

⊗ The paper used in this publication meets the minimum requirements of the American National Standard for Permanence of Paper for Printed Library Materials Z39.48-
1984.

To all the women and the men in museums
who try to "make a difference"

Contents

Contents

Contents

Foreword

A DISCOURSE on gender issues in museums must include testimonials, accounts of role models, and descriptions of model exhibitions and programs. While there are a significant number of curators who have exhibited sensitivity toward gender representations, there have been few pathbreaking exhibitions. Additionally, the tangible effects of equal opportunity employment and inclusive policy-making in museums remain elusive. In exploring gender equity, it is imperative that museum professionals examine both positive and negative organizational and educational models, because in shaping behavior, establishing new policies, and presenting new images, we must be both analytical and self-critical.

During a recent discussion with museum educators in southern California, I was asked to identify my mentors. Many of the participants assumed that they would be primarily female museum educators. During the early years of my career, however, my mentors were not from the museum community. They were male and female community leaders and educators and exemplary models, who never imposed limitations upon myself or others because of race, age, or gender. They were also good listeners and effective communicators; but more importantly, they were people who were willing to share power as well as responsibility.

As a child growing up in the fifties, I attended public schools in which the teachers were generally women and the principals were all men. My grandfather pastored a church where the deacons and trustees who helped with management were men and the dedicated church supporters and fundraisers—the "willing workers"—were women. My doctors were men who were assisted by women nurses, and most of the other authority figures in my life were also men.

This pattern of men in positions of leadership was evident when I entered the museum profession in 1976. I worked in an education department in which most of the educators were women and the Vice Director for Education was male, as were the other directors. Most of the art and history museum directors that I met outside my job were men. I often met women who directed children's museums and alternative art centers; however, very few directed the larger history, science, or art museums. Many fledgling cultural workers were not socially conditioned to question this situation, for it was the prevailing model in most communities.

The women whom I did encounter in leadership positions were often de facto leaders—strong, personable, and memorable. Many were senior administrators in museum directors' offices. They were often power brokers and problem solvers and were usually intermediaries between employees and their directors. Others were department heads and mid-level managers. Those who stood out were diligent, highly organized, solution-oriented individuals.

There were, however, informal organizational models that I believe have shaped the management skills and performance of men and women in museums. Throughout my education experiences, I had many teachers and professors—mostly women—who empowered my fellow students and me to grow and to learn in a structured and nurturing environment, teaching us work habits that enabled us to meet measurable goals. Educators on every level have imparted organizational skills, oral and written communication skills, and leadership styles that have informed behavior in the workplace.

Informal organizational models are also found in the family context. The first board meetings that I attended were run by my grandmother. A formidable and visionary leader, she was able to state the issues clearly, while also giving each family member an opportunity to be heard. She had no patience for whiners, and she looked askance at pontificators who "beat the dead dog to death." At the conclusion of her meetings, all knew what action was expected of them and when they were expected to deliver.

During my early years as a museum educator, I was so pleased with my work and my environment that I initially gave little thought to women's status in the workplace. I became acutely aware of the inequities when a colleague who was negotiating a pay raise was informed that she did not need one because she had a husband. As a single mother raising two children, I wondered how my needs would be interpreted.

Since that time, I have often heard the suggestion that museum educators and docents are wealthy men's do-good spouses who, having nothing else to do, volunteer or take low-paying jobs in education. This erroneous impression demeans and demoralizes the many women who bring commitment and dedication to the field.

I have recently served on several selection committees for senior-level positions in a variety of museums. One of the issues that became apparent to my colleagues and myself was that while men often had both advanced degrees and substantial work experience, women with children usually had either one or the other. When considering applicants for government employment, we discovered that because women in their thirties and forties were less likely to have served in the military, they were adversely affected by the veteran's preference and were thus less likely to get a position than a man of the same age with comparable experience.

However, while childbearing may interrupt or limit the careers of some women, it can create opportunities for others. I was privileged to work in a museum in which many of my colleagues loved their work and had bonded with the museum's collections and community. The staff was exceedingly loyal, and turnover was low. When positions did become available, it was often because a female staff member had gone on maternity leave and had chosen not to return, or because a spouse had relocated for better employment opportunities. As more institutions begin to offer family leave, and greater attention is given to child care as a responsibility of both parents, there may be a shift in institutional behavior, resulting in greater equity in employment opportunities.

During the seventies I watched many male educators and curators at small museums be commandeered to move furniture, drive trucks, and clean supply rooms. Young male high-school interns often complained that female interns were assigned to office work, while they were sent to the craft shops or the maintenance crews. Assigning tasks based on perceived gender roles is so pervasive that it affects the treatment of volunteers, visitors, and consultants.

Many museums have hired female art handlers, some of whom were challenged by male artists who doubted their ability to lift or carefully handle works of art. Most museums have fully diversified their guard forces, and a few have done so with their carpentry, electrical, and mechanical shops. However, few men have been assigned work traditionally performed by women. At the Smithsonian Institution most of the security guards are men who have served in the military—many as clerks, procurement officers, fiscal officers, and secretaries. It is very difficult for them to make a transition from the security force to administrative positions.

Our need to establish work cultures where people are not hampered, limited, or stereotyped because of their gender mandates that we analyze every aspect of a museum's use of human resources. Whether it is our governing boards or our security forces, we have an obligation to assess our current employment practices to identify trends that reveal discriminatory behavior. We are also obligated to overcome these behaviors by actively diversifying our work forces.

In exhibitions and public programming, we need to view our work with a more critical eye by examining it from perspectives that are different from our own. We must be aware of and eliminate language, visual context clues, and inferential meanings that distort and misinform because of limited conceptions of gender roles.

We must be open to ongoing evaluation, and we must be prepared to implement change.

Claudine Brown

Preface

*If I were asked . . . to what the singular
prosperity and growing strength of that people
[the Americans] ought mainly to be
attributed, I should reply:
To the superiority of their women.*
Alexis de Tocqueville[1]

THE ESSAYS in this volume make no claims to the "superiority" of women in the museums, but reflect a cross section of female and male perspectives on feminist issues in museums of yesterday, today, and tomorrow. The contributors share their experiences, examine women's historical role in museums, identify the forces of change, assess the scholarly and educational impact and influence of women, and prescribe and predict a feminist future. The contributors were not chosen because they all reflect similar views; indeed, the wide range of attitudes represented include the conservative, the moderate, and the militant. But neither unanimity nor conflict is the purpose of this volume.

The feminist movement in the United States during the early seventies bypassed the museum community. More accurately, American museums have ignored the feminist movement since its inception. Sufficient numbers of women necessary to make it a cause célèbre may not have existed at the time, or few men neither saw women's status in museums as a problem nor believed that an alleged "old boy's club" did exist. Unfortunately, there are few statistics to substantiate claims of sex discrimination. The Susan Stitt study of almost twenty years ago did establish that very few women were in leadership positions in museums and that women's salaries were lower than those of their male counterparts. Through informal data and personal observations and experiences, however, women are now more aware of contemporary shortcomings and inequities in the museum field. There is a renewed activism, and the status quo—particularly the elite male image of museums—is being challenged and affected. The term "feminism" now has a different connotation. No longer possessing a radical image, feminism has become both a positive intellectual force to be reckoned with in museums and more acceptable among museum professionals.

Despite imbalances, women have played a major role in founding and leading museums, as well as in scholarship and education, since the nineteenth century. Recognition from their male colleagues has been slow. Their skills, perspectives, talents, and expertise are often overlooked, while those of men are emphasized. Women are thus disadvantaged in the decision-making process and in the competition for professional leadership positions in major museums.

Although unprecedented opportunities for women exist in museums, there are still inequities: lack of institutional initiatives to deal with sexism; not enough change in women's status in leadership positions and in research and scholarship; and general indifference to feminist issues in museums. The lack of data and statistics are problems when trying to set priorities and to find solutions. There is, however, a guarded optimism among this volume's contributors.

In "Pioneering Efforts of Early Museum Women," Kendall Taylor refers to Jean Weber's presentation at the 1986 Smithsonian Institution conference, "The Changing Roles of Women in Museums," to delineate the three generations of women in the museum profession in the United States: "those who began museum work before the close of World War II and in the years up to 1950," who "were either highly specialized or had become associated with museums through prior involvement in a related field;" those, tending to be generalists, who entered the field between 1950 and 1970 during a period of major expansion in museum activity; and those working from 1970 to the present, who have had advanced academic and professional training and see museum work as a professional career, and often as an alternative to university teaching.

Four years later, in "Changing Roles and Attitudes," Weber suggests a fourth generation of women emerging in the museum field that is aware of "burnout" and unrecognized overachievement. This group is increasing in number and has practical concerns about retirement plans, overtime pay, physical and ethical safeguards in the workplace, realistic job descriptions, and an agenda of goals instead of dreams. It is becoming common for women to be as persistent as men in demanding basic safety nets for performing in the workplace and in advocating a feminist agenda. Women's parity in museums is not enough.

Lois Banner, in "Three Stages of Development," suggests that during the past twenty years, feminist scholarship in each discipline has moved through a three-stage process: emphasis on documenting both discrimination and liberation; identifying and investigating separate female traditions and cultures; questioning the theoretical bases of all the disciplines; and studying men more directly in gender studies. How do these theories relate to museums? Specifically, there has been a general neglect of women as theorists and interpreters of the visual arts in historical terms in art museums, where women have addressed the popularization and socialization of art rather than promoting its aesthetic values. In general, however, even though there are now more exhibitions developed by and about women (not necessarily women's history), the new feminist scholarship has yet to be incorporated into collections and exhibitions. History, a deliberate construction by a particular individual or group, looks at the past to understand, to interpret, and to give meaning to the present. In "A Case Study of Applied Feminist Theories," Barbara Clark Smith shows how she applied a feminist approach to produce the exhibition, "Men and Women: A History of Costume, Gender, and Power," for the National Museum of American History. According to Smith, such an approach affected her interpretation of the objects, causing her to reassess the accepted history and to reexamine the exhibit's audience, ultimately to construct a female audience through design and interpretation.

A statistical review of the present situation of women in museums reveals, for example, that there are about thirty-three women in the Association of Art Museum Directors and only three African Americans among its membership of close to two hundred. There are one-hundred-fifty women directors out of a total of fourteen hundred art museums in the United States. Although a woman was one of the founders of the Association of Science and Technology Centers, it took eighteen years for it to elect a woman president. The American Association for State and Local History appointed its first woman director as it celebrated its fiftieth anniversary. In 1994 the American Association of Museums has a woman president for the first time in its eighty-seven year history. Recognition of women as leaders in museums' professional associations continues to be slow.

In "The Empowerment of African American Museums," Rowena Stewart asserts that it was a woman who started the movement for African American museums, which empower black people to select their own heroes and to control the depiction of their heritage, struggles, and social contributions. As the ferment for gender equity increases, there will be a similar impetus to construct and to interpret the histories of all women.

According to Ann W. Lewin in "Empowering the Mind of the Child in Children's Museums," there is relatively little gender bias in children's museums, because they explore fundamental learning concepts: "How do I think, and how do I make this work?" Some 85 to 90 percent of the founders and directors of these museums are women, serving as role models to steer their programs away from stereotyping the sexes.

In "Bringing Civility to Science Museums," JoAllyn Archambault states that the role of women in science museums is that of civilizers, as female researchers bring their expertise and added virtues of nurturers and socializers. No longer will there be exhibitions of "boys and their toys" but ones that are oriented to the social realities of our system, thus dealing with all human beings.

As the United States approaches the twenty-first century, there are already signs of a profound restructuring of society, institutions, and lifestyles. Museums, long regarded as mere preservers of the past, must also become barometers of the future. How successfully they adapt to the rapid changes inside and outside their walls will determine their own futures. The same is true for women. Facing both increasing threats and opportunities, women have to construct a preferred future—perhaps one that is quite different from their past or present. Women have been the echoes of men. The true woman as a complete individual in her own right is a dream of the future, but we are making progress. Women in museums can choose to remain silently exploited, to compromise, or to confront reality and to create museum spaces of their own. Women may hope to flourish in the society of the future, but prejudices die hard. To confront them, they must present a point of view and even take chances and risks. Gender will make a difference, and the real question may be how museums respond to unavoidable social change. Women have a public ear now, and it is crucial that their arguments for appropriate positions in society not be merely self-serving.

Women will thus have a special role in museums as social reformers once again. As museum education becomes a top priority, the role of the museum educator—traditionally a women's role—will become enhanced and more respected. Women may thus have primary control over the content and the interpretation of exhibitions of social and environmental relevance that address serious community problems.

There is a renewed zeal within the feminist movement for scholarly and thoughtful gender equity in museums. Leadership is the key if it achieves consensus and unites people—both activities that women perform well. Women must educate themselves in technology and entrepreneurship, discuss the issues with their colleagues, expand their networks, become mentors, and ask pertinent questions. They must also become more politically aware in terms of media in order to be successful in the next decade. These issues are popular, as readers devour books by such feminists as Gloria Steinem, Johnetta B. Cole, Susan Faludi, and Nan Robertson.

Museums are not there to sell the future but to enable people to make better decisions about the future. Women need to be exposed to good feminist theory as it relates to museums of the future, to actively apply it, and to be alert for signs of progress. The goal is for women to be active in museums as fully as possible. Women have the responsibility in the nineties and into the twenty-first century to make a difference. As society and the world change, women must also change—with wisdom, integrity, and their own visions for the future.

NOTES

As a direct result of the 1990 seminar on which this book is based, a group has been organized at the National Museum of American History, Smithsonian Institution, to consider gender equity in exhibitions. It has produced a slide program, "Toward Gender Equity in Exhibitions," with specific suggestions for changes. The basic premise is: "about one-half of all people are women. Does the museum fulfill its mission (. . . an educational institution dedicated to understanding the experiences and aspirations of all people of the United States . . .) of understanding women? How can museums best understand and express women's experiences and aspirations?"

1. Alexis de Tocqueville, *Democracy in America,* ed. Phillips Bradley (New York: Vintage Books, 1969), 2:225.

Acknowledgments

THE ESSAYS IN this volume resulted from presentations at a March 1990 national seminar, "Gender Perspectives: The Impact of Women on Museums," at the Smithsonian Institution in Washington, D. C. Thirty-two panelists and about two hundred participants explored and discussed the past, present, and future situations of women in museums. Each of the seminar's sessions had a particular focus and outstanding women and men as speakers, responders, and moderators—some providing prescriptions, and others offering challenges as they provoked lively, intelligent, and straightforward discussions.

The seminar was chaired by Jane R. Glaser and coordinated by Artemis A. Zenetou, both of the Smithsonian Institution's Office of the Assistant Secretary for Arts and Humanities. Working with a pan-Institutional steering committee, the seminar's stated goals and objectives were: to examine women's historical impact on museums; to share experiences that show how gender perspectives have a significant effect on museums' scholarly and educational pursuits; to identify societal and technological changes in museums that affect women; to assess scholarly, educational, and leadership roles for women as museum professionals; and to look to museums of the future for the effect of gender perspectives.

Four years earlier, the Smithsonian Institution and the Ford Foundation sponsored a national conference, "Women's Changing Roles in Museums," which was timely and relevant to women's concerns during moments of potentially dramatic social, cultural, and technological changes in museums. The broad issues discussed at that conference were concerned with women's roles in a changing society, which were also evident in museums. From the 1986 conference, the idea for the 1990 seminar was born to pursue the issues and to focus on women as museum professionals, whose influence on research, collections, exhibitions, publications, and education programs is potentially enormous but not always acknowledged, recognized, or welcomed. The insightful presentations of the 1990 seminar far exceeded its goals and objectives and bear witness to the challenges facing museum women into the twenty-first century. We are extremely grateful to the speakers whose essays appear in this book, as well as to Alice Green Burnette, Assistant Secretary for Institutional Initiatives, who graciously introduced the seminar's keynote speaker, Mary Schmidt Campbell.

We thank the members of the seminar's steering committee who graciously provided their time, energy, and expertise: James Early, Assistant Secretary for Public Services, Smithsonian Institution; Hilde Hein, associate professor of philosophy, Holy Cross College (formerly visiting researcher, Institutional Studies, Office of the Assistant Secretary for Arts and Humanities, Smithsonian Institution); Edith P. Mayo, curator, Division of Political History, Department of Social and Cultural History, National Museum of American History, Smithsonian Institution; Harriet McNamee, curator of education, National Museum of Women in the Arts (formerly program coordinator, Resident Associate Program, Smithsonian Institution); Ruth O. Selig, special assistant to the Assistant Secretary for Sciences, Smithsonian Institution; Ellen Sprouls, special assistant, National Air and Space Museum, Smithsonian Institution (formerly chair of the Smithsonian Institution Women's Council and producer of educational and public programs in the Albert Einstein Planetarium, National Air and Space Museum); Roslyn Walker, curator, National Museum of African Art, Smithsonian Institution; and Kendall Taylor, Academic Director, Museum Studies and the Arts Program, Washington Semester, American University.

The Smithsonian Institution acknowledges and appreciates the generous support of the Ford Foundation. A debt of gratitude is owed to the following offices of the Smithsonian Institution for financial support or services provided: Office of the Assistant Secretary for Public Services, Educational Outreach Fund; Office of the Assistant Secretary for Arts and Humanities; Office of the Assistant Secretary for Sciences; Office of Information Resource Management; Visitor Information and Associates Reception Center; Resident Associates Program; Office of Fellowships and Grants; Office of Conference

Services; Office of the Treasurer; and Office of Printing and Photographic Services.

We owe special thanks to Ralph Walker, Office of Information Resource Management, Smithsonian Institution, for his assistance with desktop publishing; George Robinson, Office of the General Counsel, Smithsonian Institution, for his counsel and assistance "above and beyond"; volunteers Pauline Blumenstock, Melissa Smith Levine, and Marjorie Wilkov for their enthusiasm and commitment; John C. Rumm, project director, Smithsonian Institution Traveling Exhibition Service (formerly assistant editor, Joseph Henry Papers, Smithsonian Institution), for his insightful comments; Diana F. Cohen, exhibit writer and editor, Office of Exhibits Central, Smithsonian Institution, for her perceptive editing advice; Daniel Goodwin of the Smithsonian Institution Press, who guided our preparation for this volume; and Cheryl Anderson, also at the Press, who graciously reviewed the essays in this collection.

Many other people, too numerous to mention individually, contributed ideas, time, and expertise to make both the seminar and this collection of essays a reality. We greatly appreciate their contributions.

Introduction

Breaking the Cycles of Exclusion
Mary Schmidt Campbell

MY EARLIEST consciousness of gender roles came twenty years ago, when I lived in the then relatively new African nation of Zambia. Known as Northern Rhodesia in its colonial period, Zambia had gained its independence in 1964. My husband and I arrived in 1969 to teach at the Nkumbi International College, a school for southern African refugees. Southern Africa at that time was still colonized: Mozambique and Angola, by the Portuguese; Zimbabwe, by Rhodesians; and South Africa, by the Afrikaners. Zambia was an anomaly and its independence celebrations were still new—full of passion yet reflective of a time of collective communal values.

In the midst of this environment, our first son was born in 1970, and herein lies the story of my earliest and most dramatic encounter with what I now believe is an imprisoning sense of gender inherent in the modernist idea of the independent American woman. The experience occurred in October 1970, on the eve of the Zambian celebration of independence. Every student at our school participated, and part of their custom was to dance through the streets and knock on every door, at which time the residents were expected to come out and to join the celebration. When a jubilant band of students—male and female—knocked, my husband and I went to the door. I was holding my son, who was then about five-months old, clutching him protectively in my arms. To my shock, the noisy group lifted him out of my arms and then passed him from one to another as they celebrated their "future" incarnate. For them, every child was a potential leader. But I did not see it that way; I was startled and alarmed, and felt as though my son had been taken from me. Like any good American mother, I had an intense sense of proprietorship. This was *my* child. Clearly my individualist values had clashed with the community's values, and that episode was only the beginning.

Throughout our stay in Zambia, our students would knock on our door and announce that they had come for the child. The young men would take him to their barracks and would sing songs to him or would walk him up and down the road, or the women would come and take him to their compound to comb his hair or to bounce him on their knees. As he grew older, the African teachers would come to our house unannounced, lift him on their shoulders, and take him to the local bar to hang out. To this day, my son is an exceptionally easygoing, gregarious person.

But the point is not his social development but rather my never fully accepting the African sense of communal collective responsibility. For me, having a child was primarily an act of individual responsibility.

What does this have to do with gender issues? I think that the way I had clung to my son as a young American woman in Zambia is symbolic of the way women in the United States cling to their individual achievement. As I read the essays for this volume, I was struck by the extent to which this independence and individual achievement is a leitmotif. I hear it in Kendall Taylor's essay, "Pioneering Efforts of Early Museum Women," which discusses the outstanding women who founded and directed museums—such as Mrs. John D. Rockefeller at the Museum of Modern Art or Gertrude Vanderbilt at the Whitney Museum of American Art—as well as intellectual forces such as Margaret Mead or Adelyn Breeskin. The same is true of Heather Paul's essay, "Preparation for the Future," which points to the increasing destabilization of marriage and to the needs of single parents. As an African American woman, I am proud of the individual achievements of black women museum founders and directors, which are documented by Rowena Stewart in "The Empowerment of African American Museums." Also, feminist scholarship in art history, literature, and science has unearthed histories of individual success, which have been extremely important. I share in the pride of every one of these women. But what I would like to suggest is that our emphasis on the individual may ultimately hinder our full flowering as museum professionals, intellectuals, and scholars.

I do not suggest that we should curtail our quest for excellence or the quest for that "meaningful contribution," but I do think that in the relentless striving to distinguish ourselves, we must be aware of larger communal values and goals. After all, the very purpose of a museum in the Western world is to give institutional shape to collective as well as individual values.

I will explore ways to avoid the limitations imposed by avid individualism—first by discussing community responsibility in broad terms, and then by suggesting that there may be limits to specialized scholarship. I will also explore the systemic constraints of race, poverty, and class. I believe that our own good fortune is circumscribed by these constraints.

COMMUNITY RESPONSIBILITY

If there is one experience in my career that taught me the value of community responsibility, then it was my ten years as the executive director of the Studio Museum in Harlem, a black fine arts museum in central Harlem that today collects, interprets, and exhibits the artifacts of Africa and the African diaspora. The Studio Museum in Harlem's original intent was to be a space for the working artist, hence the name "Studio." The radical change in the museum's mission offers a classic example of the intervention of community values and the force of history. The museum was founded by members of the junior council of the Museum of Modern Art and its goal was, in the spirit of the sixties, to be an integrated museum (why the council did not start with the Museum of Modern Art itself remains an unsolved mystery). The junior council brought its ideas and aspirations for integration and social utopia uptown, and in 1968 opened the museum on 125th Street and Fifth Avenue above a liquor store in a quaint loft, which had no heat in the winter and no air-conditioning in the summer. Its opening was just months after the assassination of Dr. Martin Luther King, Jr., and in the midst of great turmoil not only in Harlem but also in inner-city communities throughout the country such as Watts, Newark, Detroit, Washington, D.C., and Chicago. There was civil unrest in the inner cities for numerous and complex reasons, including the compelling need to assert a cultural identity and to define a distinct African American heritage within American society. Throughout the country, the seeds for cultural institutions were planted in storefronts, lofts, and church basements: the Dusable Museum of African American History in Chicago; the National Museum of African-American Artists in Boston; El Museo del Barrio in New York City; and the African American Museum in Los Angeles.

The original intent of the Studio Museum in Harlem was worthwhile; however, it proved to be in the wrong place at the wrong time. What is striking about the museum's history is the extent to which the aspirations of a time, an era, and a history superseded individual goals, such as those of the Museum of Modern Art's junior council. To add to the immediate historical imperative, Harlem had a spectacular history. In the twenties and thirties Harlem was a black cultural mecca, attracting poets, artists, intellectuals, and musicians from all over the world. That history was still alive in the sixties, because men and women who had lived it were around to bear witness. Romare Bearden, Jacob Lawrence, and the musicians who had played uptown could still recite vivid stories about Harlem's vibrant cultural past.

When the junior council's version of the Studio Museum in Harlem opened in 1968, it was met with immediate, emphatic, and vocal opposition from the community. From the time it opened its doors, Harlem's collective voice opposed the museum's original intent. During its first decade, the museum's mission, bent by the force of the community opposition, developed in a way that its founders had never envisioned.

The legacy of the Studio Museum in Harlem and hundreds like it (many of which have disappeared) was that they reflected the cultural needs of a community. Each of them, of course, benefited from extraordinary individual leadership, but that leadership was almost always without the financial support given by the founders of older museums such as the Whitney Museum of American Art, the Museum of Modern Art, or the Solomon Guggenheim Museum, or earlier institutions such as the Metropolitan Museum of Art or the American Museum of Natural History. Younger museums like the Studio Museum in Harlem were more reliant on their communities. I believe that the legacy of the 1960s, in all of its radical permutations, has been a shift from the museum as a preserve for a few private, well-heeled individuals to an organization geared toward accommodating many communities and constituents.

I would like to describe the lessons I learned from my experiences as a woman museum director. When I first arrived at the Studio Museum in Harlem, I saw an opportunity to realize my personal ambition to become an art historian and a curator. The Studio Museum in Harlem was a vehicle through which I could establish a professional presence. Encouraged by the fact that I had one other staff person (we were the only art historians with advanced degrees at the museum, and I was the only person who also had museum experience), I developed what can only be called an overwhelming sense of hubris that exaggerated my value in relation to most aspects of the museum. No program, no exhibition, no catalog, and no administrative or financial decision was too inconsequential to escape my attention. I paid dearly for my egotism. After two years, I was flat on my back with pneumonia and exhausted, but worse—I had a staff with little to do and a museum with virtually no professional staff depth.

It was after those two years, just before the Studio Museum in Harlem was given a 60,000-square-foot building, that I made a pivotal career decision. I had up to then considered myself as absolutely indispensable; however, I would from then on perceive myself as ultimately replaceable. Psychologically, I believe that it is hard for women to accept that. Those of us who are bright and smart and who have been distinguished are sometimes imprisoned by a debilitating superwoman myth, and thus have difficulty believing that someone else can do the job as well. I have news for all of us: there is probably not only someone who can do the job as well but also someone who can do it better.

What does that mean for us? As women in leadership roles, our job is to become mentors, teachers, taskmasters, trainers. At the Studio Museum in Harlem my first liberation came when I hired a deputy director, Kinshasha Conwill, with the intention of training her to replace me. I remember my exhilaration when I won a Rockefeller Fellowship in the Humanities, which would require a seven-month leave of absence, and the joyous feeling I experienced to know that I was able to leave the museum in good hands. As the museum hired curators, registrars, development directors, and comptrollers, I worked closely with each but always toward helping to develop their autonomy.

After ten years, when the time came for me to leave, I was comforted in knowing that I was not only leaving behind my personal accomplishments—the catalogs, the shows, the major grants—but also a proficient staff and someone prepared not only to fill my shoes but also to make her own pair, as she embarked on her own career journey. It was like learning to let go of my son in Zambia and let someone else take care of a responsibility of monumental importance.

My museum work is a lesson to everyone that they should stop working alone all the time. Recent Harvard University research suggests that group study is the way to better grades. I think the same is true for better museums. My experience is that great shows need not only great curators but also excellent curatorial teams.

Another limitation for women has been the area of specialized scholarship. The late Richard Feynman, Nobel laureate in physics, once suggested that the very process of education itself is one of specialization, whether it's the study of matter at the molecular level or the study of women's cultural and intellectual contributions. When the subject matter has been excluded from the traditional scholarship there is a time of peril when it must be studied in depth, documented, and discussed, if only to build a body of literature that previously had not existed.

In my own studies of black American art, this was certainly the case.

Whether it was the sculptor Melvin Edwards, the painter Sam Gilliam, the Harlem Renaissance, the art of the 1960s, or Romare Bearden, I found that the details of the art and the artists were available only in the most perfunctory form. The risk of course for those of us who specialize in nontraditional areas is that our work will be viewed as narrow and parochial, and indeed, if I were to critique some of my earlier writings on Bearden, I would say that they do tend to isolate his achievements from the body of American art. In fact, it wasn't until I had left the Studio Museum in Harlem to join the New York City government, where I attained a broader view of the city's cultural life, that I began to understand how power, politics, and culture were ineluctably bound in the production of art. Then I began to situate Bearden's art and life within a larger context. I felt a bit like the students in the film *The Dead Poets Society,* when their teacher invited them to stand on their desks so that they could see the world from a different vantage point. When I changed perspectives, I realized that Bearden's story was not just about a black artist who grew up in Harlem and became successful; rather, it was about the symbolic struggle of race, class, and culture in this country—a struggle fought to this day with intensity and desperation.

At some point, we all have to stand up on our desks to see how our work fits in the larger scheme. Is it earth-shattering? Is it a path to a new paradigm, as Thomas Kuhn describes the route of scientific revolutions? Is it a footnote or commentary? If it is a new way of seeing an era or a discipline, then I am concerned about specialized scholarship, whose scholars are often called on to speak only on behalf of the segment of knowledge they represent and not the whole. When I worked as Commissioner of Cultural Affairs for New York, "the cultural capital of the world," I was asked to address such topics as cultural diversity or women's issues. The *New York Times* interviewed me on Spike Lee's film, *Do the Right Thing,* but never asked me about the public's funding of the arts, even though I headed an agency second only to the National Endowment for the Arts. Thus, as a result of my experiences, I believe that not only must we refuse to be limited by our specializations, but also we must not allow others to limit us. I plan my schedule with great vigilance to make sure that I have reserved time to speak on behalf of the special interests of women and black artists.

Perhaps the most egregious limitation of individualism is the systematic racism and sexism that underlie all discussions of women, museums, and the future of both. I am often asked, "How does it feel to be the first black Commissioner of Cultural Affairs for the city of New York?" I respond that my being the first has nothing to do with me but with the failings of a democratic society. If our society still finds it noteworthy that someone with my training, experience, and background has achieved the "high" status of a city bureaucrat, then we are in deep trouble. Our expectations are low, the results of which are everywhere evident.

Our low expectations are especially evident in museums. As commissioner, I was stunned to see the extent to which our museums are almost obsessively homogeneous, exhibiting little cultural or gender diversity in their boards, senior staff, museum directors, programs, audiences, and attitudes. Since museums are like artifacts, they reveal in their structures the deep cleavages among us that continue to persist. I believe that every museum director who does not have a diverse staff, every board chair who tolerates unintegrated boards, and every public official who gives public funds to these institutions is contributing to the continuing disaffection of many Americans. Women in museums who are looking for responsibility and who truly want to lead museums into the twenty-first century must decide today to make a contribution toward change, to break these cycles of exclusion.

I believe now that I have learned a lot since my earlier "independence celebration" at the Studio Museum in Harlem. I would like to have been in Zambia with my son, who is now a senior in Swarthmore College, and for him to have seen Nelson Mandela step off the plane and embrace Kenneth Kaunda, the president of Zambia. I am in a much better position now to understand the meaning of the collective joy that had embraced my son twenty years ago, and how ultimately liberating it can be to assume responsibility far beyond our individual boundaries.

PART 1

The Impact of
Women and Museum Work

A Historical Perspective

THE HISTORICAL context for the complicated subject of gender perspectives and women's impact on museums is important in providing a broader picture in which to locate our specific and detailed concerns. It is also important in giving us a perspective on ourselves. In what ways is our situation unique and in what ways not? Are we just following a path already taken, or forging ahead in new directions?

For instance, it occurred to me that the history of women's participation in museums—in their establishment and management—paralleled the rise and progress of reform movements in this country. During the first part of the nineteenth century, when art was regarded as exerting a civilizing influence on society as a source of refinement and morality, museums were advocated as necessary institutions in social education. Women became involved in the development of museums at this time as an aspect of the philanthropy they were or had already practiced, such as the abolition, temperance, women's rights, and prison reform movements, as well as all the other movements within what came to be called "freedom's ferment." By 1860, however, professionalization and the establishment of specialized societies restricted the attractions of the museum to the public, and museums that remained general in their scope abandoned their educational function and emphasized entertainment as did, for instance, the museum of P. T. Barnum. Women also abandoned their interest in developing museums, as the museum lost its social purpose, and not until the late nineteenth, early twentieth century—during the period of progressive reform—did they resume their efforts. Under the impact of progressive interest in improving the environment and expanding educational opportunities, women began to become active in the widespread movement to establish museums in communities throughout the country and to bring to the people the best they could find in art, science, and history.

The establishment of museums in this nation owes a great deal to women's efforts, which are continuing today. The relation of these efforts to present-day reform interests is clear and looks promising for the future.

Lillian B. Miller

Pioneering Efforts of Early
Museum Women

Kendall Taylor

JEAN WEBER, in her presentation, "Images of Women in Museums," given at the 1986 Smithsonian Institution conference entitled "The Changing Role of Women in Museums," hypothesized three generations of women in museums. The first generation was those who began museum work before the close of World War II and in the years up to 1950. These women—people such as anthropologist Margaret Mead and art historians Agnes Mongan and Adelyn Breeskin—were either highly specialized or had become associated with museums through involvement in a related professional field. A second generation of women entered the field between 1950 and 1970, when there was great expansion in museum activity. They tended to be generalists, rolling up their sleeves and performing the numerous activities that needed to be done in the expanding museum profession, such as organizing collections, renovating buildings, and developing public programs.[1] A third generation of museum women entering the profession from 1970 to the present has been university trained—many with master's and doctor degrees—and has viewed museum work as a bona fide profession. In many cases, this generation benefited from the retirement of large numbers of museum people during the sixties and seventies and viewed museum work as an attractive and intellectually respectable alternative to teaching and other activities in the humanities field.[2]

More has been written and discussed about this most recent generation of women museum professionals than the first two groups. For that reason, I have chosen to concentrate on those women who actively contributed both to the museum profession before 1960 and to the advent of the women's liberation movement. Other essays in this book examine in detail the effects of that cultural and societal revolution on the museum profession.

Because the emphasis of America's early museums was educational, and because women were associated with education and had long served as elementary school teachers, they naturally gravitated toward museum education programs. From this position it was also natural for them to become involved in the founding and staffing of children's museums. However, in the museum field, during the first half of the twentieth century,[3] curatorial and directorial positions usually went to men with advanced degrees and specialized training, just as the majority of college and upper-level teaching positions were filled by men. Women with higher degrees were still oddities in the early twentieth century, more often than not unmarried and thus nonconformist in their decision not to follow the traditional female role.

Because women often lacked the necessary credentials, they were also viewed as generalists and amateurs—enthusiastic in their endeavors but not truly professional. In museums, professionalism meant having highly specialized training, and before 1960 only a small percentage of women had that. When women did pursue advanced degrees and obtain higher positions, they often lacked the degree of authority given to men, which was necessary to perform leadership jobs. Not only were professional relations with male superiors more difficult for such women, especially when they did not share the male point of view, but also relations with other women on the museum staff were often strained, since the success of a few women in the mainstream was threatening to other women who maintained their traditional roles.[4]

The majority of women in museums played the same role as most women in the domestic sphere: supporters of male counterparts. Men were the heads of households and the heads of institutions; they made the rules and set the tone at both home and work. Women fulfilled men's directives, tidied up, and kept the records, which is why so many of them later entered registrar departments. In addition, until the women's liberation movement, upper-class and well-bred women often volunteered at museums. For married women, especially those who married well, there was a stigma in accepting compensation for cultural work.[5]

With the women's movement of the sixties and the subsequent surge of women to graduate schools, as well as the alteration in attitudes toward their paid employment in museums, women's involvement and role in the museum profession changed. Women with similar degrees and experience began to compete with men for the same jobs—creating a whole new ball game.

These new women professionals, however, had forerunners who had paved the way, establishing women's professional credibility in the museum field through their dedication and competence. It is these early women that this essay examines. As pioneers in the museum field, during the first half of this century these women were founders, directors, and curators of some of America's most important museums.

Since the early 1900s women have played an important role in founding major museums. As collectors and benefactors, they helped to build some of America's most prestigious institutions, including the Isabella Stewart Gardner Museum in Boston and the Havermeyer wing at the Metropolitan Museum of Art in New York. For example, Ellen Scripps Booth and her husband, George Gough Booth, were founders of both the Cranbrook Academy of Art and the Cranbrook Institute of Science. Anna Hills, a prominent artist during the twenties, organized and developed the Laguna Beach Art Association, the forerunner of the Laguna Beach Museum of Art. Sarah Cooper Hewitt and her sister Eleanor Cooper Hewitt, daughters of Abram Hewitt, mayor of New York in the 1880s, founded the institution now called the Cooper-Hewitt Museum of Decorative Arts and Design.

Significantly, almost all the major museums started by women in this century are arts-related: the Museum of Modern Art was founded by Lizzie Bliss, Mrs. Cornelius J. Sullivan, and Abby Aldrich Rockefeller; the Folk Art Museum at Colonial Williamsburg was also founded by Rockefeller with the assistance of Edith Halpert; and the Whitney Museum of American Art was founded by Gertrude Vanderbilt and Juliana Force. Most recently, the opening of the Strong Museum in Rochester, New York, exhibits the eclectic collecting passions of its founder, Margaret Woodbury Strong.

The Museum of Modern Art, now affectionately known as MOMA, was conceived by Rockefeller and Bliss to spotlight the avant-garde. Meeting by chance during the winter of 1928–29 in Egypt, where both had gone to escape the cold New York weather, they discussed launching a modern art museum. On the way back to New York by ship, Rockefeller shared the idea with another fellow traveler and friend, Mary Quinn Sullivan (the wife of Cornelius J. Sullivan) who thought it a splendid notion. Once back in New York City, "the ladies" (as they came to be known by the trustees and museum staff) went into action. They raised money, garnered support, and opened the doors to their new museum just ten days after the stock market crash of October 1929.

And who were these women? Mrs. John D. Rockefeller was the former Abby

Greene Aldrich, daughter of the powerful Senator Nelson W. Aldrich of Rhode Island. Lizzie Bliss was the spinster daughter of a successful textile merchant who had briefly been Secretary of the Interior under President McKinley. She was a close friend of the artist Arthur B. Davies and was involved in the organization of the 1911 Armory Show. Bliss also had one of the finest collections of modern French and American art in the United States. Finally, Mary Quinn Sullivan was the wife of a successful attorney, Cornelius J. Sullivan, who had a large and lucrative New York City law practice. Together they enlisted the financial aid of A. Conger Goodyear, making him president, and hired as the museum director the brilliant twenty-nine-year-old Alfred Barr, Jr. The Museum of Modern Art was on its way, as Rockefeller went on to help found the Folk Art Museum at Colonial Williamsburg, hiring Edith Halpert to assemble a cross-section of American artifacts to be used to restore Williamsburg as a colonial town. The artifacts were installed there in 1940. Halpert also later assisted Electra Webb in forming a folk art collection that was donated to start the Shelburne Museum in Vermont.

Perhaps the most successful of women founders of an art museum was the team of Juliana Force and Gertrude Vanderbilt Whitney, daughter of Cornelius Vanderbilt II, one of the richest men in America, and also the wife of Harry Payne Whitney. Their partnership worked extraordinarily well over a period of forty years. Force was a champion of young artists eager to bring their work to the attention of the public but without the funds to do so. Whitney, herself a sculptor, had the same desire but not the organizational skills nor the time to do the job. In spite of their differences in wealth and social position, Force and Whitney shared some important qualities with each other: good taste, a quality of bohemianism, a willingness to take risks, and an appetite for new experiences. At the beginning, Force primarily served as Whitney's secretary, shielding her from outside demands. In 1908, however, Whitney delegated Force to begin buying and exhibiting the works of artists not recognized by the New York dealers. By 1930 Whitney had converted her New York City studio, at 8 West Eighth Street, and the house next door, then known as the Whitney Studio Club (a membership organization for young artists), into nine galleries that were capable of exhibiting more than nine hundred paintings. The opening announcement of the museum emphasized the women's goals:

> At the present time there is no museum in America devoted exclusively to the American fine arts, and it is in part to fill this gap in the ever-growing lists of American museums that Mrs. Whitney has founded a museum of American art. Museums have had the habit of waiting until a painter or a sculptor had acquired a certain official recognition before they would accept his work within their

sacred portals. Exactly the contrary will be carried on at the Whitney Museum of American Art.[6]

With Force as director from 1930 until her death in 1948, Whitney saw her hopes for supporting American artists come to life. Force also benefited greatly from her position. Besides directing the museum, she also became a trustee of the American Federation of Arts and, during the Depression, held an important government position as New York regional chief of the Public Works of Art Project (PWAP).

One of the recent American museums to be founded by a woman is the Strong Museum in Rochester, New York, which contains the extraordinarily broad and diverse collection of Margaret Woodbury Strong. Reflecting her wide interests and fascination with both decorative and utilitarian objects, the Strong Museum—which opened to the public in 1982, ten years after it was founded—traces the acquisition interests of the founder from the twenties, when she first began collecting seriously, until her death in 1969. Committed to have her museum "make sense" to visitors, Strong gave her executors the latitude to transform what could have become a static collection into a dynamic one. She gave the museum sole discretion to determine what portion of the estate "if any would be required to provide a perpetual endowment fund including provisions for the acquisition of additional appropriate collections for display of interest to the public."[7]

Whereas most of the women who founded museums were actively involved in hiring directors to run their institutions, few ever considered that role for themselves. In the first half of this century, when women were hired to spearhead institutions, the majority turned out to be very successful. Beatrice Winser of the Newark Museum is a perfect example. She was a woman who might have been labeled a "whizbang." Described by many as "the busiest woman in Newark, New Jersey," and one of "the steam engine women of the state,"[8] she directed two of Newark's largest institutions, the Newark Public Library and the Newark Museum, guiding them through the Depression years. For fifty-three years she was on the staff of Newark Public Library, succeeding John Cotton Dana as director after his death, also assuming the other post Dana had held—that of director of the Newark Museum.

Winser, the daughter of a newspaper man at the *New York Times,* was born in Newark in 1875 and studied at Columbia University. She was an unusual woman of outstanding ability, and John Cotton Dana recognized that early. At thirty-three, Winser was already assistant director of the library when Dana came to Newark, and during his tenure at the museum, she was his right-hand woman. Between the two there was mutual respect and deep friendship.

Together they made the Newark Museum a lively and important force in the community. For them, the museum's major role was educational; a museum was intended to be an institution of visual instruction, a concept that was only gaining currency at the beginning of this century. According to Dana and Winser, "a good museum attracts, entertains, arouses curiosity, leads to questioning—and thus promotes learning."[9] Winser never wavered from that philosophy, and for years the Newark Museum stood at the forefront of America's museums. After Dana's death, Winser, following Dana's wishes to make the Newark Museum of greater service to Newark, opened branch museums in various sections of the city, including branches in the public library and in Bamberger's department store.

The Newark Museum stood out in another major way. For almost forty years after Dana's death in 1929, all its directors—Winser, Alice Kendall, and Katherine Coffey—were women, as well as a majority of its key personnel. Thus, the museum led the way both with its progressive philosophy regarding the role and function of the museum in the community and with its foresight in hiring capable women to serve as heads of major cultural institutions. Coffey was so effective in her role as museum administrator that since 1972, as a tribute to her legacy, the Northeast Museums Association, now the Mid-Atlantic Association of Museums, annually presents the Katherine Coffey Award to a preeminent professional in the museum field. Coffey, a Barnard College graduate, was curator at the Newark Museum prior to becoming its director and, in the tradition of John Cotton Dana, educated a whole generation of students by continuing museum work of the highest standard and quality.

Although women museum directors before the forties were rare, they were not unknown. Some highly capable ones from this earlier period include Cornelia B. Sage Quinton, director of the California Palace of the Legion of Honor from 1924 to 1930, who began her museum career in 1904 as assistant secretary of the Buffalo Fine Arts Academy; Mary B. Thayer, director of the Art Institute in Omaha during the twenties; Mary Cooke Swartout, director of the Grand Rapids Art Gallery, who in 1932 became the director of the Montclair Art Museum in New Jersey; and Robina Rae, director of the Red Cross Museum in Washington, D.C., from 1929 to 1948. Another highly capable woman director, Margaret Wall, head of the Suffolk Museum at Stony Brook, New York, which she joined in 1945, contributed greatly to the establishment of that museum's collection of the American genre paintings of William Sidney Mount, a long-time resident of Stony Brook. Under Wall's direction, the Suffolk Museum at Stony Brook acquired a national reputation that attracted competent future women directors such as Susan Stitt, who directed that museum for more than a decade.

Perhaps one of the best-known women directors during the twenties and early thirties was Laura M. Bragg, head of the Charleston Museum. A graduate of Simmons College, Bragg edited the *Charleston Museum Quarterly* until 1931 and was chairperson of the Southeast Museums Conference. A keen thinker as well as an excellent speaker, she presented a carefully developed proposal on cultural museums and the use of cultural materials at the opening session of the twentieth annual meeting of the American Association of Museums (AAM) in St. Louis on 18 May 1925. In this speech she advocated the use and interchange of cultural material to create better understanding among nations, saying that

> people are always going to fight, but with our knowledge of disharmony, we also know that the better people understand each other, the better they are able to smooth out their difficulties. Now a piece of Chinese porcelain can be used to create an understanding of the Chinese—sympathy toward their point of view in regard to things.[10]

So great was the female community's esteem for Bragg during her tenure at the Charleston Museum that in spring of 1923 the women of Charleston presented her with a watch, saying

> Miss Bragg has done noteworthy work at this time, when the women's movement has the attention and is demanding the thought of men and women all over the earth. Realizing and appreciating this, the women of Charleston are deeply grateful that their banner is carried by a woman of the type of ability and character of Miss Bragg . . . that our cause is in such worthy hands.[11]

Grace McCann Morley's career in museums was equally notable. Her professional activity spanned seven decades from 1930, when she joined the staff of the Cincinnati Museum as curator, until the eighties, when she received the AAM's award for distinguished service. In those years she served as director of the San Francisco Museum of Art, the first head of the museum division of the United Nations Educational, Scientific, and Cultural Organization (UNESCO), and one of the creators of the International Council of Museums (ICOM) and *Museum,* the first publication to define and explain principles of museology to both developed and developing countries. She received her B.A. and M.A. from the University of California. She then spent three years studying abroad at the University of Grenoble, the École du Louvre, and the University of Paris, where she received her Ph.D. In the thirties, when she moved to San Francisco from Cincinnati, she found herself in the right place at the right time; the San Francisco Museum of Art, a remnant of the Panama Pacific Exposition of 1915, was looking for a director. Housed on the top floor of the Veterans' Building near City Hall, the museum determined its primary focus to be American contemporary art. Morley specialized in American art, furniture, and decorative arts, and the board of trustees thought she suited the job perfectly. The museum opened in January 1935 with Morley at the helm, and she stayed there, with time off for other duties, until 1958. After 1959 she lived in New Delhi, India, working as the director of the National Museum of New Delhi, which she headed until 1966. Her decision to spend her later years in India was based on her desire to share her knowledge about museological principles with developing nations and to train them in preserving and interpreting their heritage, so as to make it meaningful to the population.

Another art museum, the Baltimore Museum of Art, has had a long history of women directors. Florence N. Levy, the founder and longtime publisher and editor of the *American Art Journal,* was the first director of the museum from 1922 to 1926. She had previously been a staff member of the Metropolitan Museum of Art in New York from 1900 to 1917, where she mounted exhibitions of works by Winslow Homer, William Merritt Chase, and James McNeill Whistler. A graduate of the National Academy of Design in New York City, from 1909 to 1915 she was secretary of the School Art League in New York City and a leader in its work of promoting art education in the city's public schools. She was called upon during World War I to direct the activities of the Art Alliance of America, which provided designs by American artists to manufacturers who previously had depended on European designers for their supply. This brought her work to the attention of the trustees of the Baltimore Museum of Art, who chose her in 1922 to develop their new museum in the Garret Mansion on Cathedral and Monument streets and to adapt the structure to the museum's needs, tasks to which Levy was well-suited. She responded enthusiastically and was successful in realizing the Baltimore museum's challenge to become "a place where everyone will find a cordial welcome—to school girl and boy and their teacher, the silversmith and the locksmith, the painter and the collector, as well as the public at large."[12]

Adelyn Breeskin came to the Baltimore Museum of Art in 1930, four years after Levy had left, and seventeen years later became its director. In the early thirties she helped to organize its department of prints and drawings, later becoming general curator in 1938 and acting director in 1942 (by her own admission, as a result of World War II). She remained director until 1962, transforming the institution into a nationally prominent museum.

Born into a well-to-do Baltimore family (her father was Alfred Dohme, founder of Merck, Sharpe and Dohme Chemicals), she recognized a love for art early and pursued an education in art, architecture, and design at Harvard University, Radcliffe College, and Boston University. She began her career in 1918 as an assistant in the print department at the Metropolitan Museum of Art, where she first encountered the work of Mary Cassatt in the form of drypoint prints, and went on to become the foremost expert on Cassatt's work.

Breeskin was fond of saying that without the occurrence of World War II, she would never have obtained the directorship at the Baltimore museum. That was certainly the case at the Virginia Museum of Fine Arts in July 1942, when the museum's directorship was taken over jointly by Mrs. John Garland Pollard and Beatrice Von Keller, formerly head of the art department at Randolph-Macon Woman's College. Mrs. Thomas C. Colt became the museum's acting secretary of membership and extension. In addition to creating a female wartime staff, the museum's board pushed to have the museum's programs continued and popular programs intensified to strengthen public morale. Other museums across the United States did the same, and many women obtained their first jobs in museums during World War II.

Many women also entered the museum profession as a result of the children's museum movement. As Melinda Young Frye pointed out in her 1986 presentation, "Women Pioneers in the Public Museum Movement," at the Smithsonian Institution conference, two of the AAM's charter members were influential figures in the founding of children's museums.[13] When the AAM was founded in 1906, two of its initial members were Delia Griffith, then director of the Fairbanks Museum of Natural Science in St. Johnsbury, Vermont, and Anna Billings Gallup, who was involved in the 1899 founding of the first children's museum in America, the Brooklyn Children's Museum in Brower Park. Gallup was an insightful, early museum educator who quickly saw the educational potential of museums and set the stage for the emergence of other children's museums around the nation.

Gallup received her B.A. at Massachusetts Institute of Technology, teaching biology before joining the staff of the newly founded Brooklyn Children's Museum in 1902. By 1904 she had been appointed curator of the museum, a position that she held until 1937. Griffith, one of the AAM's charter members in 1906, was greatly influenced by Gallup's work in Brooklyn. She began her educational career as director of nature studies in the public schools of Newton, Massachusetts, becoming director of the Fairbanks Museum of Natural Science in 1903. She later helped to found the Boston Children's Museum, becoming its director in 1913 and remaining there until 1925. She then founded and became the first president of the Children's Museum of Hartford, which she directed from 1927 until her retirement in 1946.

Louise Condit was yet another museum professional to be influenced by Anna Billings Gallup. After receiving her M.A. in elementary education from Columbia University in the thirties, she took her first position as supervisor of education at the Brooklyn Children's Museum, working under Gallup for two years. Because of this association with Gallup, Condit has always been considered a link to the start of the children's museum movement in this country, as well as one of the pioneers of museum education. At the Brooklyn Children's Museum,

> she endlessly pursued the discovery and development of children's interests, and the children's museum was a beehive of after-school, weekend, and vacation activities. Every possible space was used for clubs, activity labs, or workshops, and there were always opportunities for puzzles and games, bird walks, field trips and auditorium programs.[14]

While many of these activities had objectives similar to today's science and technology centers, they emphasized supervised group activities, because exhibits then were generally simple and homemade, and children could not be left unattended as often as they are at today's more sophisticated and interactive discovery centers.

The children's museum movement quickly gathered momentum as the Depression declined, with museums for young people being founded throughout the nation. Two well-known ones were started by Gertrude Gillmore in Detroit and Grace Golden in Indianapolis. The success of the Indianapolis Children's Museum is partially due to Golden's thirty-six years of devoted leadership. She came to the museum in 1928 when it occupied a three-room, downtown apartment. Under her steady guidance in the thirties and forties, it was transformed into one of the foremost children's museums in the world. Creating a whole new concept of museum display, Golden developed portable exhibits that circulated among Indianapolis's and surrounding school systems. At her retirement in 1964, more than fourteen hundred display cases were being rotated among schools. In 1964 the institution's executive secretary, Mildred S. Compton took over, taking the museum from its then turn-of-the-century house to a new, multimillion dollar building that opened in 1976. In the twenty-one years that Compton served as director, from 1964 until 1982, she

spearheaded the dramatic transformation of the museum from a small institution serving an audience primarily composed of the city's school children, to the
world's largest children's museum, reaching primarily a family audience of well
over one million each year. In order to bring the museum to this point, she did
all of the things museum directors need to do: build a strong board, a broad
base of financial support, a commitment to long-range planning and a core of
professional standards for the museum itself.[15]

A widow and mother of two small children when she came to the museum,
Compton held a B.S. degree from the University of Michigan and an M.A.
from Tulane University when she arrived in Indianapolis. From 1940 to 1946
she had worked as a chemist at Eli Lilly and Company and taught at Sophie
Newcomb College.

Like museum directors, museum curators or "keepers," going back to the
origins of the English term, have been predominantly men. That slowly started
to change in this century as women pursued advanced degrees to obtain the
same professional status as men with similar educations. Women curators in
the scientific fields, making the first breakthroughs as anthropologists, zoolo-
gists, archaeologists, ethnologists, paleontologists, and ichthyologists, paved
the way. But curators in the liberal arts soon followed and were aided by circumstances precipitated by World War II.

Catherine Lemmon Manning, known as "the first lady of philately," was
curator of the Smithsonian Institution's division of philately almost continu-
ously from 1912 to 1951. She arrived at the Institution when the U.S. Post Office
transferred its stamp collection to the Smithsonian. Besides being curator of
the massive collection, she wrote many articles about collecting stamps and
was an active member of the Washington Philatelic Society. Considered one of
the nation's foremost stamp experts, Manning was a Washington, D.C., native
and an avid stamp collector since her early youth. She received numerous
awards for her expertise.

Another curator concerned with paper was Dorothy Miner, who belonged
to the first generation of American women museum professionals that received
advanced academic training in art history. Her career spanned almost forty
years, in which she served as curator of manuscripts and rare books as well as
curator in charge of Islamic and Near Eastern art at the Walters Art Gallery in
Baltimore. In four decades she established a reputation as an outstanding
scholar in manuscript studies and book arts, lecturing part-time at Johns Hopkins University and publishing over ninety articles and commentaries.

Miner was exposed to museum work throughout her upbringing. Her father, Roy Miner, joined the American Museum of Natural History in 1905 as

assistant curator of invertebrate zoology and in 1922 was appointed curator of marine biology. He was a charter member of the AAM and was present at its first meeting in 1906. He encouraged Dorothy to pursue a classics and English degree at Barnard College, where she graduated Phi Beta Kappa in 1926. From there she went on to graduate work in art history under Meyer Shapiro at Columbia University, where he was just beginning his brilliant scholarly career. Dorothy Miner's success as a curator and scholar, in part derived from her writing ability, was exhibited primarily in essays concerning works in the Walters collection. She would define an object and make it come to life. Her discussion of various types of vellum is a good example:

> Medieval Italy liked vellum crackling; Germany and England preferred it suede-like and thick; France made it so thin it was semi-transparent. One can almost tell the general region of origin of a book by one's fingertips so much does the texture of the vellum vary, particularly in the centuries before the Renaissance.[16]

Miner's position at the Walters Art Gallery enabled her to concentrate her efforts on the study of medieval manuscripts. Her work in that area resulted in her both devising inventive ways to pursue those studies and demonstrating a spontaneity and enthusiasm not often found in serious scholarship. Like many other professional women of her generation, Miner never married. Her job was her life, and her insistence on approaching each manuscript as a cultural artifact with a fully integrated physical structure helped set the groundwork for future programs of codicology.

Although female curators in arts-related fields were more prevalent during the thirties and forties than earlier, it was in the field of natural sciences that the greatest strides by women professionals were made. Named after Mary Jobe Akeley and her husband Carl, the Akeley African Hall at New York's American Museum of Natural History is a tribute to the couple and contains numerous materials collected by them. Mary Akeley was a geographer, explorer, mountaineer, and author of many books and articles recounting her adventures around the world. She made her first trip to Africa with her husband in 1926, when he undertook what was his fifth African expedition to gather data for the American Museum of Natural History. At that time they had been married for only two years, and on the trip Carl Akeley became ill with fever in the mountains of the Congo and died. Mary Akeley insisted (against the museum's wishes) on remaining in the Congo, then a Belgian colony, to complete his work. She buried him at Mount Mikeno, took charge of the expedition, and photographed mountain gorillas and other animals to complete his research on animals in their natural setting. In 1927, when she returned to New York City, the museum named her as adviser in the development of the African Hall.

Born Mary Lee Jobe in Ohio in 1878, she had had a superior education, first graduating from Scio College in Alliance, Ohio, and then enrolling at Bryn Mawr College for graduate work in 1901. She taught history at Temple University in Philadelphia and at Hunter College in New York, and almost a dozen years before marrying, had established herself as one of the world's leading women explorers. An avid mountain climber, she made several expeditions to explore the Canadian Rockies and two Canadian mountains are named in her honor: Mount Jobe and Big Ice Mountain. Throughout her life (she died in 1966), she continued to involve herself in zoological and ethnographic studies in Africa, writing about tribal people, particularly the Zulu and the Swazi, and encouraging the establishment of game preserves.

In 1926, the same year that Mary Jobe Akeley was in Africa collecting materials for the American Museum of Natural History, Margaret Mead was beginning her own career at that museum as assistant curator of ethnology. Having just returned from her first trip to Samoa, Mead was beginning a career that would span fifty years at the museum—first as assistant curator, then associate curator, then curator, and finally as head of the Margaret Mead Hall of Pacific Peoples. Educated at Barnard College, where she received her B.A. in 1923, she went on to obtain her M.A. and Ph.D. from Columbia University, becoming an adjunct professor there in 1954. Her first book in 1928, *Coming of Age in Samoa*, is still considered a classic anthropological text. But her first love was always museum work, and from her earliest days at the museum, she was often heard to say that if she stayed long enough and was lucky, she might be able to "do" a hall. Mead got her wish. In her final days at the museum she occupied a sixth-floor tower complex that overlooked the future site of the Margaret Mead Hall of the Pacific Peoples.

Ethnology, anthropology, paleontology, archaeology—these were museum fields in which women were becoming more prevalent during the twenties and thirties. For example, Winifred Goldring became associate paleontologist at the New York State Museum in 1925; Francesca LaMonte was hired as associate curator in the department of fishes and aquatic biology at the American Museum of Natural History in the late twenties; Marie Wormington became the first archaeologist to work for the Denver Museum of Natural History in 1935, and following her, Arminta Neal became curator of anthropology there as well as assistant director. Neal also wrote two highly successful museum studies books, which are still used internationally: *Help! for the Small Museum* and *Exhibits for the Small Museum*.[17]

Yet while making inroads into the professional ranks, women curators continually had to struggle to change the attitudes of the predominantly male directors who hired them. Nancy Lurie, curator of anthropology and section head of the Milwaukee Public Museum, is an example. She was the first woman ever hired to head a scientific section in that museum and paved the way for other female scientists. Recalling her first years there, she spoke of an incident involving the male head of taxidermy. At the museum only a few months, she asked if she could watch him make a cast of a snake:

> I asked what kind it was and he said, "An asp, the kind that bit Cleopatra." Then with a leer, "Do you know where it bit her?" For once my head was working, and I answered sweetly, "In Egypt." After that he was quick to say that the museum should have started hiring women scientists long ago.[18]

Initially as a result of World War II, another branch of the natural sciences—zoos and zoological parks—also saw the entrance of women into its professional ranks. In 1943 the Seattle Zoo at Woodland Park hired two women as keepers: Margaret Wheeler and Melvina Kuempel. In the same year, the Barrett Park Zoo on Staten Island hired the first female zoo veterinarian: Patricia O'Connor, a 1939 Cornell University Veterinary College graduate. O'Connor had wanted to become a zoo veterinarian since her childhood, and a reminder of her frequent visits to zoos as a youngster was a small scar on her hand, the result of a lion's scratch. She got her wish and spent a productive career caring for animals and conducting biology courses in connection with the zoo's educational programs.

Bella Benchley is another well-known zoologist. She joined the staff of the San Diego Zoo in 1925 as bookkeeper, and in a few short years became the world's first woman zoo director. In 1940, with fifteen years of zoo experience behind her, she wrote a book entitled *My Life in a Man-Made Jungle*, recounting numerous experiences—some humorous, some tragic, and others thrilling—about her work.[19]

While women were making advancements as curators in the sciences, they were also contributing greatly to the development of regional museums. As Melinda Young Frye pointed out in her presentation, "Women Pioneers in the Public Museum Movement," at the 1986 Smithsonian Institution conference, women played an important role in the development of this nation's regional museums. The Oakland Museum in northern California is a prime example. Although developed by a male curator, the Oakland Museum experienced important early development under associate curator Daisy DeVeer and directors Suzie Mott and Alice Mulford. (Mott directed the museum from 1920 to 1945. When Mott died in 1946, Mulford took over.) Frye emphasized that

Oakland's experience was significant because it symbolizes the dedicated and enlightened efforts of women museum leaders throughout the early decades of the 20th century to make a success of their institutions, sometimes against great odds. . . . They did battle at City Hall; cajoled local merchants into donating supplies and providing advertising; dreamed up, researched, designed, and installed changing exhibits; coordinated school programs; and lectured to special groups in the museum. They planned budgets, raised money, wrote annual reports, hired and fired, and generally managed to keep the flame alive and the educational mandate flourishing.[20]

The mandate for education and excellence was also clearly evident in the work of America's early female art curators. As we have previously seen with women involved in the founding of museums, the art world has long attracted the interest and commitment of women. Three well-known and respected art curators and supervisors, spanning three generations in this century, are Emily Millard from the Corcoran Gallery of Art and Dorothy Canning Miller and Riva Castleman from the Museum of Modern Art.

Millard, born in 1880, was manager of special exhibitions at the Corcoran from 1910 to 1948. In 1939 she served on the advisory committee of the New York World's Fair and, as her obituary noted, "was an untiring advocate of women's place in the administrative field of art."[21]

Born some twenty years later, Dorothy Canning Miller in 1943 became curator of painting and sculpture at the Museum of Modern Art (MOMA), one of the first women art curators in the nation. She organized a series of controversial exhibitions of contemporary American painters and sculptors, which introduced the work of Jackson Pollock, Mark Rothko, Clyfford Still, Morris Graves, Mark Tobey, Louise Nevelson, Jasper Johns, Robert Rauschenberg, and Robert Indiana. A graduate of Smith College, where she majored in art, Miller got her start in one of John Cotton Dana's training programs at the Newark Museum. While there, she impressed one of her teachers, Holger Cahill, who used to take the students to see artists' studios in New York City. When Cahill was later asked to temporarily replace Alfred Barr, Jr., as director of MOMA, he hired Miller to help him. Cahill stayed only one year, then left to head the Work Projects Administration (WPA), and married Miller in the interim. Her longevity at MOMA was greater than Cahill's; she began doing curatorial work there in 1934 and stayed until the seventies.

It was in the mid-seventies that Riva Castleman joined MOMA, becoming director of the department of prints and illustrated books in 1976, and later becoming deputy director for curatorial affairs, a position she still holds. A Chicago native, she has her B.A. in art history from the University of Iowa and completed graduate work at the Institute of Fine Arts at New York University. Well-informed, educated, and experienced, Riva Castleman is typical of the scores of highly competent women curators who presently hold influential positions in museums around the country.

How far have we come? Agnes Mongan, formerly director of Harvard's Fogg Museum, partially answered this question in a *Museum News* interview. Asked if she were aware of any qualified women in the museum field who had not been advanced simply because they were women, she spoke of dining rooms in an anecdote that asks us to read between the lines:

> My sister was curator of prints and drawings at the National Gallery of Art from 1941 until about seven years ago. There was a special dining room for the staff, and the men had it designed for themselves. She said she went to the front of the line the first day she was a curator. Even fairly recently, and it still may go on, women weren't welcome in the special dining room at the Museum of Fine Arts in Boston. A famous curator, who is as knowledgeable in her field as anyone, was at the MFA a great many years, and she was never in the staff dining room.[22]

Mongan's anecdote dates to 1975, and while much has changed in the past years, much hasn't. Although women today do compete on an equal basis with men for most museum positions, once in those jobs their advancement is often slower than men's. The present generation of women museum professionals is changing that, and the generation that follows will continue these efforts. As we have seen from the women discussed, women's acceptance as equals in the field has been a gradual process—one which has yet to reach its final conclusion.

NOTES

1. Jean Weber, "Images of Women in Museums," in *Women's Changing Roles in Museums,* ed. Ellen Cochran Hicks (Washington, D.C.: Office of Museum Programs, Smithsonian Institution, 1986), 21–22.

2. Kendall Taylor, "Risking It: Women as Museum Leaders," *Museum News* 63 (February 1985): 20–32; and Kendall Taylor, "To Create Credibility," *Museum News* 69 (July-August 1990): 41–43.

3. Research for this essay involved the review of early issues of *The Museologist, Museum News,* and other museum-related journals and periodicals. Eileen Shapiro, a graduate of the George Washington University Museum Studies Program, assisted with this research. Additional information was acquired from a questionnaire sent to museums and historical societies that inquired about the role women historically have played in their institutions.

4. Jean Weber, "Images of Women," 23.

5. Ibid.

6. "Whitney Museum," *The Art Digest* 4, no. 7 (1 January 1930): 9.

7. Carol Sandler, "Margaret Woodbury Strong—Collector," Strong Museum, 1989, 14.

8. Letter from Richard C. Jenkinson to James A. Robertson, 3 August 1927, cited in Barbara Lipton, "John Cotton Dana and the Newark Museum," *The Newark Museum Quarterly* 30, nos. 2 and 3 (Spring-Summer 1979): 34.

9. John Cotton Dana, *The Museum* 1, no. 2 (April 1925).

10. Laura M. Bragg, "Culture Museums and the Use of Culture Material," *Museum Work* 8, no. 3 (September-October 1925): 82.

11. "Laura Bragg Honored," *Museum Work* 6, no. 1 (May-June 1923): 38.

12. "Baltimore's New Museum of Art," *Museum Work* 5, no. 5 (January-February 1923): 90.

13. Melinda Young Frye, "Women Pioneers in the Public Museum Movement," in *Women's Changing Roles in Museums,* ed. Ellen Cochran Hicks (Washington, D.C.: Office of Museum Programs, Smithsonian Institution, 1986), 11–16.

14. Robert W. Ott, and Gillian Greenhill, "Museum Education Then and Now: Reflections by Three Pioneers," *Museologist* no. 165 (Fall 1983): 5.

15. Remarks by Tom Leavitt about Mildred Compton on the occasion of her receiving the 1988 AAM Distinguished Service Award at the 1988 AAM meeting.

16. See Claire Richter Sherman, "Pioneers in American Museums," *Museum News* 59, no. 5 (March-April 1981): 40.

17. See Arminta Neal, *Help for the Small Museum: A Handbook of Exhibit Ideas and Methods* (Boulder, Colo: Pruett Publishing, 1987); and Arminta Neal, *Exhibits for the Small Museum: A Handbook* (Nashville: American Association for State and Local History, 1976).

18. Letter from Nancy Oestreich Lurie, curator, Anthropology, Section head, Milwaukee Public Museum to author, 13 October 1989.

19. Bella Benchley, "My Life in a Man-Made Jungle," *Parks and Recreation Journal* 24, no. 3 (November 1940): 110.

20. Frye, "Women Pioneers," 16.

21. "Emily Millard, Leader in Art, Is Dead at 72," *Washington Post,* 31 March 1952, sec. 2B.

22. "Pioneers in American Museum: Agnes Mognan," *Museum News* 54, no. 1 (September–October 1975): 33.

Influence and Effect

Paul N. Perrot

WOMEN'S RELATIONSHIP to museums has been critical from the very beginning. None of our institutions could have operated without the volunteer services that women have provided, nor without the stability, continuity, sense of quality, dedication, and learning that they have and continue to provide as staff. An ongoing problem is that there are so few statistics on women's role that indicate the kinds of positions in which they are employed, the differential between men's and women's titles, and, more significantly in a materialistic society, the patterns in women's promotion that differ from those of men's. Is our gratification for women's contributions adequately recognized or reflected in the level of their renumeration? In short, a disparity continues to persist between the salaries given to men and those given to women. In the future real progress will not occur or endure unless some of our shortcomings, indeed injustices, become history, and men, as part of the problem, are awakened to the recognition that their existence as professionals would be totally impossible without the contributions of women.

I have met a number of outstanding women in the museum field who have exerted a major influence on my life and career. For example, the formidable—in her learning and sometimes in her presence—Gisela Richter at the Metropolitan Museum of Art for over fifty years developed the museum's classical collection. Richter built on the foundation established by her predecessors, who had accumulated a vast collection; however, she oriented the classical collection toward the direction that it finally took. Equally if not more important were her well-respected publications on Greek classical art. When she retired, her assistant Christine Alexander inherited her position and continued to give scholarly prominence to the department.

There are other women who have been influential in the museum field. Those include Dorothy H. Dudley and Irma Bezold, whose book on the manipulation, preservation, transmission, and recording of objects in collections, as well as the extraction of information from them has proven to be invaluable to our endeavors. Their extraordinarily useful guide, *Museum Registration Methods*, was published some twenty years ago and is in its third printing.[1] Women have also made strides in conservation, a fundamental aspect of our profession. Caroline Keck, who founded the Training Center at Cooperstown, was instrumental in convincing museum professionals of its importance. She is also one of the great "persons"—and I am using "persons" in the sense that we are not alluding to gender—who have influenced me. One of the attributes of the great women museums professionals is that they know themselves to be leaders who have a mission, and they are able to convey this—if not impose it—upon their male counterparts.

I think of the museum profession's lesser-known figures such as Margaret Freeman, who was assistant curator at the Metropolitan Museum of Art and who supervised the Cloisters during the collection's development. She was also instrumental in creating the programs that transformed that great oasis of medieval art into the international center that it has become. This would not have occurred without Freeman and the close relationship that existed between herself and James Rorimer, the director. Perhaps their relationship today would be a little different, but there was certainly the sense of two persons working together for a common cause.

Another woman museum director who has had a strong influence on me was Gertrude Moore, the second director of the Memorial Art Gallery at the University of Rochester. With her sister Isobel, she directed the gallery for nearly a half century. It is in her administration that a very important collection was developed, with modest funds and a rare sense of connoisseurship.

Other influential museum women include Kathryn Buhler at the Boston Museum of Fine Arts, whose studies of American silver and silver in general have become the cornerstones upon which further scholarship in this field has developed; Gertrude Townsend, curator of textiles at the Museum of Fine Arts; and Edith Standen at the Metropolitan Museum of Art, who knows more about tapestries than anyone else except the people who originally made them. These women helped me realize from the very beginning that, indeed, there should be no gender distinctions made in our profession. Thus, I attach great importance to the essays in this book, hoping that they will lead not to a more militant attitude—because militancy sometimes is not what is needed—but to a more serious and thorough attempt at quantifying where we are now.

In 1978 the American Council of the Arts issued an *Arts Administration Compensation Survey*, which states that

> in the Chief Executive Officer position, males are consistently paid a much higher salary than females for those areas where the sample is large enough to make a valid comparison.[2]

Today, over a decade later, we are not able to measure progress because sufficient statistical information is still unavailable. Although the Association of Art Museum Directors publishes a salary survey every year, it does not categorize by gender, thus providing no means to determine if there is a differential between similar positions held by men and women. Yet those who are in the field know that there is a disparity that we need to correct. The problem is not only national but also international. A survey published in the July 1989 *Museums Journal* in England suggests that there are few women museum directors in that country. The median salary for seven women directors was £12,240, while the median for men was £18,587. If one looks at other positions, one finds in Rank 0, which is the highest, to Rank 4, which is in the middle, that there are far more men than women, while from Rank 4 to 8, which is the very lowest range, there are far more women.[3] As directors, trustees, and managers, we are shortchanging ourselves and our institutions if we do not do something about this disparity, because the final measure of respect and equality is evident in the pay scale and the promotion rate. Something needs to be done to correct this obvious discrimination against women.

Another indication of discrimination is that none of the persons mentioned by Kendall Taylor in the previous essay are minorities, and at the moment we have no statistical means to find out if and to what extent minorities continue to be unrepresented in the museum field. I see here an opportunity not to develop manifestos but, in a concentrated, cool, and collected fashion, to start demonstrating that there are fundamental inequalities in employment opportunities, compensation, and advancement, as well as basic shortcomings on the part of management in failing to recognize that by not giving every opportunity for women to rise to the topmost levels of museums, they are actually lessening the profession's ability to serve their communities.

In conclusion, there are and have been many women, particularly those in directorial positions, who are so qualified and gifted that there are no males who could have surpassed or equaled them in capacity, accomplishments, and what they have given to the museum profession.

NOTES

1. See Dorothy H. Dudley and Irma Bezold, *Museum Registration Methods,* 3rd ed. (Washington, D.C.: American Association of Museums, 1978).

2. See Mitchell B. Smith, *Arts Administration Compensation: 1978 Survey* (New York: American Council for the Arts, 1980).

3. See Phyllida Shaw, "The State of Pay," *Museums Journal* 89, no. 4 (July 1989): 26–28.

Changing Roles and Attitudes

Jean Weber

IT WAS a privilege and an important learning experience to participate in the 1986 Smithsonian Institution conference, "Women's Changing Roles in Museums." It was my first formal venture into the women's movement and my first admission that I needed gender support.

I grew up before the feminist movement, and made many critical decisions in life under assumptions that were natural for young women who grew up in the postwar forties and fifties. We were expected to get a good education, to express our opinions, and to gain respect as intelligent human beings. The proper forum, however, in which a woman could address an issue was the domestic sphere, surrounded ideally by a proud and adoring family. From that vantage point she could volunteer her talents, perhaps by serving on boards or holding office in charitable organizations. After all the children were in school, she could work part-time, and perhaps full-time when the children finally left home. My life, like that of many of my sisters of that generation, was derailed from that career track more than once. I ultimately went to work in a children's museum many years ago.

To prepare this essay, I reviewed the 1986 conference proceedings in order to measure where we had been then.[1] What were our attitudes and perspectives? What agenda had we set for ourselves? It seems that in 1986 we were mainly concerned with gaining self-confidence and full acceptance, joining the mainstream, developing survival strategies, and obtaining increased professional recognition. True to the trends of the eighties, we were self-centered, interested primarily in personal advancement. Are these still our major concerns? Has anything changed? Are we measuring our progress, gathering confidence, and applauding our successes, or are we commiserating over the same old abuses? Have we begun to share gains, extend congratulations, strengthen our ties, make new contacts, and redefine the issues? I hope that the essays in this book provide a realistic sense of where we should be concentrating our energies.

Kendall Taylor's "Pioneering Efforts of Early Museum Women" profiles early women in museums and suggests trends that drew women to the field and perhaps armed them for survival. These women seem to have been independent, masterful, determined, intense, swift of mind and sometimes of foot, and perhaps a little lonely. At the very least, they had to be capable of thriving in a solitary position. The museum field, however, is no longer a solitary environment for women, because their roles have changed dramatically, as have their expectations. There are more options for women today. The basic assumptions that I grew up with have changed substantially in just three decades. Now a young woman has a large number of legitimate and socially acceptable possibilities in choosing a life-style or a career.

At the 1986 Smithsonian Institution seminar Marc Pachter, speaking of opportunities for women scholars, noted that

> once it became allowable for women to work in an intellectual arena, they naturally came to museums because, in American society, cultural work is traditionally women's work. It is an attitude that European society considers ridiculous, but in the United States, culture was often considered frivolous. And as something frivolous it was consigned largely to women.[2]

Frivolous or not, women went to work in museums in increasingly large numbers, and by 1986, according to Susan Kalcik, women outnumbered men as professionals in the museum field and as trainees in museum studies programs. Kalcik worried about "what some have called the feminization of the museum field."[3]

In its older and pejorative sense, feminization meant lower wages and esteem. Such perceptions of museums as frivolous and of the profession as one of low esteem are directed well beyond what we call women's issues. They reflect our attitudes, not just as or toward women but also as tax-paying Americans, toward our museums. If we agree that museums were considered elitist and nonessential at the turn of the century and remained as cultural frills in the minds of some people at midcentury, it appears that there has been little change in our present society's deeply rooted attitude toward museums. Museums remain embedded among a myriad of causes, philanthropies, and challenges. The drug crisis, medical care, AIDS research, deficiencies in public education, environmental issues, and continued racial inequality all struggle along with museums for support and recognition as the worthy causes of our time. As true believers in museums and their worth, how can we place them as equals, fully deserving public support, in that breadline? Are we too ultimately victims of the prevailing attitude toward cultural institutions? If not, how do we further our cause? As women, we know what it is like to be undervalued. As women, are we not uniquely positioned to help make the case for our museums?

For the independent and remarkable pioneer women of the early twentieth century, the museum provided a suitable arena for the development of their talents and self-esteem. These women established collections, education departments, and program activities that became fundamental to the distinctive character of American museums. Women's traditional interests in education and their willingness to serve as volunteers on boards, as docents, in fundraising and auxiliary groups, and as assistants was a major factor in the increase in public involvement in museums. By the fifties women's organizations were founding children's museums, art leagues, community art centers, historical societies, storefront museums, and historic home displays. With good will, enthusiasm, and a great sense of public service, women set a fast pace in the proliferation and variety of museums and established an astounding record as preservers and interpreters of the products of our culture. But as the collections grew—sometimes indiscriminately—so did the problems.

With the next generation—composed of the housekeepers, managers, organizers, and recorders—another set of traditional women's values came into play. Women in museums, for example, began to make order out of chaos by taking what they had and improving or making the best of it. These women of midcentury found great rewards in the sacrifice and the accomplishment of taking on a dirty job and overcoming impossible obstacles. Self-esteem was not necessarily an issue, as collections were sorted, documented, and maintained.

By the time a third generation of women gathered at the Smithsonian Institution for the 1986 conference, women in museums were remarkably smart, well-trained, professionally savvy, and ready for combat as equals to men in the world of museums. They were high achievers, looking for career challenges and recognition, as well as the right to prove themselves capable of leadership positions in all kinds of museums and at all levels. To a certain extent, their plans have succeeded. The pressure to excel remains steady, and there is an increasing flow of well-qualified applicants entering the work force. They have proven that women can excel in almost any capacity in the museum environment; however, there is still an element of sacrifice—great achievement at the risk of exhaustion. Women in high positions seem to be goal-oriented and committed (occasionally driven) to produce landmark exhibitions, splendid publications, innovative programs—in short, to work miracles over and over again. The museum workplace provides no safeguards for such endeavors. It continues to exploit men as well as women who are prepared to work diligently and creatively, supposedly with the product being their principal reward. For many the career track can grind to a sudden halt with an unpredictable change of director or new board president. For others the burnout ratio is high, and personal lives often suffer.

In my own driven way, I have begun to feel the welcome breath of a fourth generation of women in the museum field. These are people who have had it with the burnout and the unrecognized achievements. They are appearing in increasing numbers in my office with practical concerns about retirement plans, overtime pay, physical and ethical safeguards in the workplace, realistic job descriptions, and an agenda of obtainable goals instead of audacious dreams. They are addressing the inadequacies of the typical museum infrastructure and the instability of several generations of charismatic leaders in the museum world. They are not begging for opportunities for individual achievement, but are expecting to find workplace conditions that are conducive to efficient and satisfying teamwork. It is becoming common for women to be as demanding as men are about the basic safety nets for performing on the job. Too often in the past men went elsewhere when faced with lack of professional stability in the field, and women gratefully took their places.

If women are finally to make the leap from the museum field to the museum profession, they will do so by addressing these mundane but critical personnel issues. What is required are good job descriptions established and accepted salary levels, standards for comparable qualifications, and a strong code of ethics with safeguards and sanctions. Clearly defined and generally accepted program and management practices benefit both men and women equally. Proper practices delineated on paper and approved by boards of trustees are genderless. Such policies should be implemented soon, because there has been a considerable redistribution in gender roles, and it is clear that both men and women are exploring these issues.

I suggest that we begin to apply to our museums the gender perspective that has been gained from several decades of wrestling with the challenges women confront in the workplace. Museums as institutions, like women as individuals, have suffered by being undervalued despite their contributions to society. Museums are enjoyed, placed on pedestals, admired, and permitted to be a little eccentric but are expected to quietly take care of their own needs and stay out of the mainstream. We have learned a lot about personal survival as women, and I think it is time to apply some of our hard-earned knowledge to assure the survival and the full acceptance of museums in our time.

NOTES

1. See *Women's Changing Roles in Museums,* ed. Ellen Cochran Hicks (Washington, D.C.: Office of Museum Programs, Smithsonian Institution, 1986).

2. Marc Pachter, "Women as Scholars: The Validity of Cultural Scholarship," in *Women's Changing Roles,* ed. Hicks, 87.

3. Susan Kalcik, "Introduction," in *Women's Changing Roles,* ed. Hicks, 3–4.

PART 2

The Impact of Feminist Scholarship

New Approaches to
History, Art, and Science

THE TOPIC of gender is particularly acute in the current literature of African art history. For over ten years, I have been investigating the depiction of gender in contemporary Baule figurative sculpture, questioning, for example, why men are clothed and women are unclothed. The questions are numerous; the answers are tentative.

I have often thought about the nature of knowledge and its acquisition. Children and young people often grow up with a charmingly naive belief that knowledge is based on objective facts that exist "out there" in the world— facts that are tangible, that one may almost trip over. A corollary belief is that explanation entails putting these "facts" together in a coherent way. How awesome and scary it is to discover later that this is not the case, and that facts only exist in response to our inquiry and come into being through our activity in the world. This topic could be called vision, which allows us to see a bigger picture and allows us to escape the limited paradigm in which women have been represented. This is also the vision that allows us to see.

Philip Ravenhill

Three Stages of Development

Lois W. Banner

THE PREMISE that the personal is political is central to feminist scholarship. In this essay, I include several anecdotes drawn from my own experience.

In 1963 I scouted the shelves of the Columbia University Libraries looking for a doctoral dissertation topic. I briefly considered and then rejected the idea of writing a biography of Lydia Maria Child, because I found that one had already been written. In 1963 the feminism of the late sixties had yet to influence me. I had not realized that a woman's life could be written about from new perspectives and that the feminist discourse would soon so powerfully reconceptualize all the older histories and biographies of women, that they would have to be rewritten.

When I wrote my dissertation on the Protestant ministry of the early nineteenth century, I found enough material on women to devote an entire chapter to them. I never considered publishing this information. Gathered almost by accident, it seemed quaint and secondary. Eventually, the topic of women and religion in this early period would become of major importance to historians of women.

In 1969, when I taught one of the earliest courses on women's history in the nation, I worried about finding enough material for an entire semester. At that point, having been trained to regard the history of men as the only history that mattered, I could not visualize how the history of women could involve anything more than the history of the women's suffrage movement. Because this topic impinged on the male world of politics that had been almost my whole course of study as a graduate student at Columbia University in the early sixties, I was knowledgeable about it. Today, after twenty years of teaching the course, I can hardly cover the richness of women's history in one semester.

During my twenty years of scholarship in women's history since 1969, I have happily demonstrated the inaccuracy of my earlier assumption that no significant history of women existed. Over the past twenty years, feminist scholars have uncovered women's history, demonstrating its protean richness. We have created, as have feminist scholars in every field, a vast expansion in our knowledge base. The experience of discovery has been glorious. Like a psychoanalyst discovering the therapeutic contours of a hidden past, I found a historical past that through my entire education to its Ph.D. pinnacle had never been revealed to me. In the beginning I could have dreamed neither of the depth of discoveries that were to be made nor the range of organizations, journals, conventions, and books that would be produced within the academy, the museum world, and the larger society.

I have been asked to focus in this essay on developments in the feminist scholarship of various fields. I do so guardedly, cautioning that my interdisciplinary approach stretches thin at the edges, when I move into fields such as the sciences or art history in which I am only peripherally involved. In these cases, my approach is based much more on what I have read rather than on personal experiences.

Nonetheless, I have discovered an exciting similarity in each of the disciplines I cover. In each area during the past twenty years, feminist scholarship has moved through a three-stage process. The first stage involved an emphasis on documenting both discrimination and liberation. The second stage was one of identifying and investigating separate female traditions and cultures. The third stage, which has emerged in the last several years, has been both more integrative and oppositional, as feminist scholars have moved to question the theoretical bases of all the disciplines and to include men much more directly as a subject of study under the rubric of "gender."

The first stage, which occurred during the seventies, was two-pronged. Initially it involved revealing the gender oppression that relegated most women to a subordinate status. Feminists in the sciences have documented the exclusion of women from laboratories and university science departments. They have analyzed gender bias in scientific theories ranging from nineteenth-century Darwinism to twentieth-century sociobiology, which defined women as secondary in evolutionary development and genetic capability. In feminist art criticism the most influential early scholarly foray was Linda Nochlin's article, "Why Have There Been No Great Women Artists?" Nochlin documents such problems as how women were excluded from the standard study of human anatomy through the use of nude models. This exclusion, which was justified on moral grounds, effectively prevented women artists from producing the allegorical and historical canvases filled with human subjects that constituted over the centuries the most critically acclaimed genre of painting.[1] Among the earliest explorations in feminist history was Joan Kelly's "Did Women Have a Renaissance?" which deals with the Middle Ages and the Renaissance. Kelly, countering earlier scholarship, concludes that the Renaissance marked a period of decline in women's status.[2] In history, Barbara Welter's "The Cult of True Womanhood, 1820–1860," which focuses on women in the nineteenth-century United States, documents women's nineteenth-century exclusion from public affairs and their assignment to the domestic sphere.[3]

In addition to analyzing the discrimination to which women have been subjected, the first stage also involved revealing women's historical participation in the arts, which resulted in the discovery of forgotten artists, writers, and scientists. In relevant fields this process of discovery also involved lobbying for the inclusion of the best of these women in each field's list of outstanding achievers or, what in literary criticism quickly came to be called "the canon." In literature, as in most other areas, this canonized list traditionally had been almost exclusively male and, more than that, Eurocentric. Feminist literary critics successfully proclaimed the greatness of Virginia Woolf, Kate Chopin, and Zora Neale Hurston. Feminist art critics rediscovered painters such as the Renaissance's Artemisia Gentileschi and the eighteenth century's Rosalba Carriera. Feminist historians of science found that Catherine Green, not Eli Whitney, had invented the cotton gin. They also found that Ellen Swallow's early twentieth-century work in sanitation, which actually provided the foundation for the science of ecology, had been classified as home economics because Swallow was a woman. Thus Swallow's name was not among the small list of women who had qualified as scientists of distinction.

Documenting oppression and liberating forgotten yet distinguished women soon shaded into the second stage: recording and analyzing women's separate experience of reality. Feminist historians especially explored and in many ways celebrated a distinct women's history. They reinterpreted women's relegation to domesticity as a source not of discriminative discontent but rather of female bonding and ultimately strength. They argued that Victorian domesticity, more than confining women, provided them with a psychological and ideological basis for liberation movements such as women's suffrage. In literature, feminist critics explored women's writings, positing that there existed a special female sensitivity and writing style that were different from those of men and that androcentric critical standards could not judge.

This period of separatism was in many ways revolutionary. The new feminist literary theories implied, for example, that entirely new standards had to be created for literary criticism. In feminist art criticism scholars challenged the standard division between a superior, male-dominated, "high" art tradition based on painting and sculpture and a debased decorative and sometimes even anonymous craft tradition that women dominated. In scholarly analyses and museum exhibitions of quilts, for example, feminist art historians and curators demonstrated that their subtle alignment of color and abstract shapes were as visually exciting and artistically important as the abstract works produced by acclaimed male artists such as Wassily Kandinsky or Willem de Kooning. In all fields the thrust toward separatism and the feminist dynamic toward social change also added a new emphasis on exploring the experience and the cultural productivity of ethnic, racial, and class groups.

Early in the history of women's studies, theorists such as Gerda Lerner and Peggy McIntosh correctly predicted the emergence of the two stages that focused on women's oppression and separatism. But they further theorized that these stages would give way to a third stage of integration. From its beginnings, feminist scholarship, rooted in the public feminist movement, was more than simply revisionist in intent. Its goal was always messianic, seeking to create what Thomas Kuhn calls in his path-breaking study, *The Structure of Scientific Revolutions,* a paradigm shift—a revisioning and recreation of the theoretical and methodological bases of all the disciplines away from their androcentric center to a gynocentric or a holistic position.[4] If feminist scholarship were to produce a full paradigm shift that would overturn male-oriented scholarship, then the center of discourse in each field had to be addressed and entirely new systems of understanding and methodology had to be instituted.

Writing when women's studies was in its infancy, Lerner and McIntosh were understandably vague as to the precise nature of the third stage. They predicted, however, that it might take many generations before the oppression of women was fully documented and women's achievements were fully revealed. The third stage, they thought, lay far in the future. Yet, ironically, it has occurred well within their own lifetimes.

Forces not specifically centered within women's studies have furthered feminist scholarship. Most important has been the widespread impact of the new postmodernist theoretical perspective within the academic disciplines, especially the humanities. Deconstructionists, post-Freudians, reader-response theorists, and even the new historicists all subject texts to intense critical scrutiny, positing, as do feminists, a dense, complex social context encircling the observable reality. By their very existence, the various postmodernist critical approaches lend credence to the companion "ism" known as feminism. They have in fact stimulated the production of numerous women's studies that explore their theoretical interconnections. Such works include Teresa de Lauretis's *Feminist Studies/Critical Studies,* as well as Irene Diamond and Lee Quimby's *Feminism and Foucault: Reflections on Resistance.*[5]

Beginning in literature, in which feminists are now calling for the end to any notion of a canon, this new integrative phase has spread to art history and to history, but has taken a somewhat different form. Like feminist literary critics, feminist art critics are calling for the end to what they regard as an androcentric and elite canon in art. They see this canon as the product of a tightly knit group of elite museum directors, art dealers, and editors of art periodicals who assume that they have the right, by virtue of their position, to dictate what constitutes "great" art. Feminist art historians focus not only on women's art and sensitivity but also on the nature of gender construction and its role in the work of both male and female artists. Writing in the *Art Bulletin,* Thalia Gouma-Peterson and Patricia Mathews cite literary critic Sandra Gilbert's model for the use of feminist scholarship. Feminist criticism, according to Gilbert,

> wants to decode and demystify all the disguised questions and answers that have always shadowed the connections between textuality, sexuality, genre and gender, psychosexual identity and cultural authority.[6]

These ideas have only recently begun to influence feminist historians. The delay, I think, stemmed not from any less commitment to change from feminist historians but from the fact that history is not a theory-driven discipline. In history the new ideas have taken the form of a commitment to "gender study," or the full analysis of the social organization of gender relations and how these relations impinge on broadly conceived historical change.

Yet here I must pause and reverse direction, because I am not entirely sympathetic to this new direction and to some of the implications of its theoretical perspectives. For example, historian Joan Scott, who is heavily influenced by feminist poststructuralists, advocates the conception of historical processes in gender studies as "so interconnected that they cannot be disentangled." According to Scott:

> We need to replace the notion that social power is unified, coherent, and centralized with something like Michel Foucault's concept of power as dispersed constellations of unequal relationships, discursively constituted in social "fields of force."[7]

The problem with Scott's theoretical position is that any notion of historical agency—of male complicity in women's oppression, or of the notion of women's oppression itself—is nearly lost.

Feminist poststructuralists have posited that the oppression of women has varied in time and within economic and ethnic groups. In practice this position has produced, on the one hand, a healthy critique of mainstream women's studies as Eurocentric and elitist. On the other hand this theoretical position supports various alarming arguments within the "men's studies" movement, which has recently emerged as a force within the academic world. These arguments focus on male oppression and sensitivity and forget male power and privilege, allowing a history to be easily written in which men are the victims and women are the oppressors.

Feminist poststructuralist arguments further coalesce in the widespread attack, especially within the discipline of history, on the venerable women's studies notion that patriarchy is an unvarying substructure that privileges men and that has existed across time and cultures. Once the concept of patriarchy is lost, I fear for the future of women's studies, because within language lies an ultimate power—the power of naming and identifying. If we are persuaded to modify our terms to achieve greater complexity and variety, we will lose the original reformist thrust of our discourse. It is no accident that, in a time of conservative reaction to the feminist movement, some of our central terms such as "patriarchy" and "feminism" are under assault.

A complex movement such as women's studies takes on many forms and variations. If gender has become a central concern to feminists in the various disciplines, they have employed gender concepts to deconstruct patriarchy. I, however, find the new theoretical perspectives from the sciences the most interesting and hopeful of all. Perhaps because the sciences remain male-dominated fields, the feminist critique within them has been especially daring and innovative. Evelyn Fox Keller has psychoanalyzed major scientists to unmask the "pretended objectivity" that she feels is the capstone of androcentric science.[8] Ruth Ginsburg has called for a gynocentric science suffused with a "feminist eros"—a sense of participation in science around the realization that each of the basic elements of scientific research (conceptualization, execution, and interpretation) involves creativity. Ginsburg believes that such creativity is not recognized partly because it is identified as female.[9] Rather than this creativity being downgraded because its joyous, erotic elements are rooted in the female, it should be celebrated.

More than this, feminists in the sciences have challenged the very thought process on which modern scientific endeavor is based. They argue that male rationality and concepts of inevitable technological progress have helped to generate our present ecological disaster and systems of social inequality. Dualistic thinking—by which culture is opposed to nature; black to white; reason to emotion; male to female—is a particularly Western form of thought that gained hegemony in the late seventeenth century during the scientific revolution. It then assumed a more holistic approach in which nature was honored and similarity, not difference, was celebrated. In her biography of Barbara McClintock, a scientist whose work on cell life was unrecognized for decades, Keller contends that women scientists used an interactive, nonhierarchical model of thinking. Keller believes that this way of thinking is especially characteristic of women's thought processes. She thus poses a separatism to women's endeavors that is reflective of the second stage of the development in feminist studies and indicates the continuing vigor of various feminist perspectives.[10]

Emerging from the thought of feminist scientists and women identified with various strains within feminist spirituality and the study of non-Western religions is a new kind of analysis called "eco-feminism." Eco-feminism combines the drive for women's liberation with respect for the environment and sees both oppressions—that of women and that of nature—as interconnected. Its emergence indicates the continuing vigor of the women's studies position and its continuing growth and development as a philosophy of social change for the liberation of both women and men.

NOTES

1. Linda Nochlin, "Why Have There Been No Great Women Artists?" in *Women in Sexist Society: Study in Power and Powerlessness,* eds. Vivian Gorick and Barbara J. Moran (New York: Basic Books, 1971).

2. Joan Kelly, *Women, History and Theory: The Essays of Joan Kelly* (Chicago: University of Chicago Press, 1984).

3. Barbara Welter, "The Cult of True Womanhood, 1820–1860," *American Quarterly* 18, no. 1 (1966): 151–74.

4. Thomas Kuhn, *The Structures of Scientific Revolutions* (Chicago: University of Chicago Press, 1970).

5. Teresa de Lauretis, *Feminist Studies/Critical Studies* (Bloomington: Indiana University Press, 1986); and Irene Diamond and Lee Quimby, *Feminism and Foucault: Reflections on Resistance* (Boston: Northeastern University Press, 1988).

6. Thalia Gouma-Peterson and Patricia Mathews, "The Feminist Critique of Art History" *Art Bulletin* 69 (September 1987): 326–57.

7. Joan Wallach Scott, *Gender and the Politics of History* (New York: Columbia University Press, 1988).

8. Evelyn Fox Keller, *Reflections on Gender and Science* (New Haven, Conn.: Yale University Press, 1985).

9. Ruth Ginsburg, "Uncovering Gynocentric Science," in *Feminism and Science,* ed. Nancy Tuana (Bloomington: Indiana University Press, 1989).

10. Evelyn Fox Keller, *A Feeling for the Organism: The Life and Work of Barbara McClintock* (San Francisco: W. H. Freeman, 1983).

Removing the Barriers to Change

Victoria Funk

MY ESSAY examines the relationship of the sciences to the three phases through which women's studies has progressed, according to Lois W. Banner's essay, "Three Stages of Development." Scientists were rather late in documenting past sexual discrimination. It was not until the late seventies and early eighties that publications mentioned this discrimination and documented the contributions that women had made to science. Lately this documentation of women's achievements has accelerated. University bookstores' women's studies shelves, for example, will have books on women in science. Because science was late in acknowledging the discrimination against and the contributions of women, the second stage actually coincided with the first stage. While women in the sciences were documenting discrimination, they were also listing women's contributions and establishing organizations to support women.

I think what we need to do now is to incorporate this information into the textbooks for freshman college classes. It is useless to have good books on women in the sciences available only for seminars and upper-level classes, while the majority of undergraduate students in biology, botany, and zoology classes use textbooks that mention only the contributions made by men. It is wrong that only in a book about women that the contributions of women scientists are found. While progress has been made, there is still work to be done. I think that pressuring textbook publishers to publish books that emphasize women's achievements in the sciences is one of the best ways to do this.

While giving seminars in both South America and in the United States, I questioned women and men in various museum and university departments about gender discrimination and received interesting responses. Of the discrimination that women face in the sciences and academia, a black woman said, "I'm very interested in knowing how many of the women in that book [on women's contributions to the sciences] are black." I thought about it and realized that this was not something I had ever even considered. I began to realize, as I talked to the students in some of the universities, that despite the discrimination that I had experienced when I was going through school, it would have been much harder if I were both minority and female.

The third phase or the integrative phase, in which the theoretical underpinnings of the various disciplines are questioned, holds the most interest for me. To preface this I would like to examine the highly competitive nature of science and research. The fight to get somewhere first and to receive credit for doing so drives the field. You have to believe that what you are doing is right and to be able to stand up and look somebody in the eye at the meetings attended by a hundred or a thousand people and say, "You're wrong, I'm right, and here's why." This is something that women must learn to do, because it is not something they are taught to do. I argued about this need with a male scientist. He said that he has been concerned with how he was raising his daughter, wondering if he was teaching her the things she needed to know. He asked me if I had played sports when I was a kid. I told him that I had played field hockey and touch football. He said, "Did you ever take your stick and knock somebody in the shins on purpose when the referee wasn't looking?" I said, "No. I never did that." Then he asked, "When you were on the line of scrimmage when you were playing football, did you ever spit in somebody's eye when the referee wasn't looking?" I replied that I had not. He responded that "boys start that when they are four," suggesting that the difference in the behavior of males and females is inherent in the way they interact with others as children. We argued for a while, and my friend said, "You know, just this morning, my daughter hit my son in the bathroom after he had pushed her, and I came in and gave her a lecture. I'm beginning to think that maybe what I ought to do is, say, 'All right, way to go.'" If male and female behavioral patterns are established at an early age, then the sciences' characteristic competitive nature makes it less difficult for men than for women to pursue.

Banner and other authors have emphasized that science is not an objective process, although scientists like to pretend that it is. It is a social process, and the group to which a scientist belongs and those who support his or her ideas and hypotheses determine how readily the scientist's ideas are accepted. This is not guaranteed, however, since most scientists enjoy debating the issues.

It has been suggested that as women continue to enter the field, things will change. Science will become more interactive, creative, and perhaps less competitive. Scientist and author Lynda Birke, however, believes that such change is not possible in our present society and that a feminist science, one run by women or having more women in it, would be geared more toward human need and would be less mystifying, because it would be accountable to society rather than to an elitist group. Birke also asks whether topics should be proscribed rather than all topics being equally open to investigation.[1] This approach concerns me, because I think that science, at least the way it is practiced, is a full-time, consuming occupation that originates from within and drives one's life. For example, sometimes when you are on the verge of scientific discovery, you can not sleep, you can not eat, and you do not want to talk to anybody. You know that you are pursuing a goal, although you may be misled. You have to be willing to take risks and to pursue it anyway—even though in ten years you may discover that you were wrong and be relegated to a footnote in the history of science. But you may be right, which is what you have to believe and push for.

Competitiveness in science is necessary. I cannot imagine the scientific process occurring around a table where a group of people sit, discuss, and arrive at a consensus. "It's my idea, I'm going to pursue it, and publish it"—that is what drives science. I am not sure what science would be like if this sense of competition were removed. My position is that all doors should be open to all people equally, and that everyone should have the same opportunities.

Having recently traveled around the United States, I can say that this is still not the case. There are schools I have visited in which, if you are trying to be a scientist and you are a woman, you are going to have a longer and harder road in graduate school. At universities women are consistently tenured at a lower level than men. Discrimination against women remains evident, not necessarily in the level at which they are being hired but at the level they are being retained. Young female graduate students are still changing advisors—two, three, and four times—before they find one that they think will treat them equally with the male graduate students.

I do not think that the practice of science has to be changed for the wrongs to be corrected and for women to be successful. We do need to make sure any excess barriers are removed and that everybody receives similar and fair treatment. Science's competitive nature is inherent in the way it is practiced, and is necessary for it.

NOTE

1. See Lynda Birke, *Women, Feminism and Biology: The Feminist Challenge* (Brighton: Wheatsheaf Press, 1986).

From Theory to Practice

Correcting Inequalities

Marcia Tucker

LET ME begin with a brief revisionist autobiography. I am the director of the New Museum of Contemporary Art, which over its sixteen-year existence, has had as its premise that art practice and art cultural conditions—their political and social contexts—are inseparable, if not one and the same. I left the Whitney Museum of American Art at the end of 1976 in a storm of controversy, after eight years as its curator. I am now one of a minority of women directors in the field but not one who was chosen to be a director. Instead, finding virtually no place for my being and my ideas within the existing museological framework, I chose to establish a museum. This made me both privileged *and* marginalized at the same time, since I had to create the institution in order to work in it.

As a student at New York University's Institute of Fine Arts, I was trained in the traditional, modernist art history mode. For many years I did not understand that there was or could be a connection between my feminism and the theoretical bases of my own exhibition and writing projects. Like so many other women in museums, I thought that what was needed was to correct inequities by simply involving women and people of color in exhibitions, criticism, and lectures, not to mention museum work itself. This period coincided with what Lois W. Banner in her essay, "Three Stages of Development," refers to as "the first stage" of feminist scholarship.

For me, this first stage meant fighting within museums to have a voice, while at the same time struggling within the larger arts community to find communalities from which collective action could be instituted. This was nearly impossible for the few women curators at the time, since most feminist artists and critics not only viewed themselves as separatists but also rejected women in power as belonging to the enemy. At this time feminist art and art criticism seemed to veer toward an existentialist bias. Women were felt to have a different experience of the world and their bodies and, therefore, were thought to create work that was different from and "better" than that of men. Characteristic of women's art were round open forms, pastel colors, images drawn from the experiences of mothering, caring, nurturing, and so forth. This was my first taste of the nature-culture dichotomy. The concept of an essential female nature caused the alarm bells to sound, at least for me, since "nature" is something that is immutable, eternal, and unchanging, while "culture" can be and most often is part of a revolution.

But if the first stage of development in feminist scholarship was hard, so was the second. Working in virtually all-male institutions, those of us who tried to include more women encountered profound resistance. Recently, when Kinshasha Conwill, my colleague at the Studio Museum in Harlem, was asked why her museum did not display the work of white artists, she replied, "Well, we certainly would, if we could only find some who are good enough!" Within the majority of museums in this country and among those possessing authority within them, women and people of color who "are good enough" are still virtually impossible to find.

The third stage of feminist scholarship described by Banner has been even more problematic for the museum profession. To take the term "integration" more literally than she intended, we should remind ourselves that today there are only forty-two women in the prestigious Association of Art Museum Directors, and there are only three directors of color among in its one hundred and fifty-three members. In the less literal sense, however, I share Banner's concern that by withdrawing the lines between men and women, by positing more fluid and open-ended notions of the social construction of gender, we will lose sight of male complicity in women's oppression and of women's oppression itself. Just as worrisome to me is the idea that men would appear to be present in feminism so as to co-opt it for themselves. Recently, listening to a learned scholar arrogantly discuss his "feminist credentials" at a panel, a friend of mine asked, "Why can't men get involved in a critique of masculinity instead of telling us how to be feminists?" Nonetheless, I believe that the lines are not and cannot be simply drawn between the two genders. I agree with social scientist Joan Scott and the many others who prefer to avoid the traditional "us-them" dichotomy created by positing men on one side and women on the other, because such dichotomies are characteristic of the Western, binary system of thought and language that shapes and solidifies inequities. Dualistic concepts such as men/women, black/white, majority/minority, and center/periphery ignore the richness of human identity and experience and perpetuate stereotypes. None of us chose our age, race, gender, or nationality; these are given. Where we position ourselves in relation to the issues, however, is very much a matter of choice.

Emphasizing men's oppression of women, which is a real factor in women's lives, also mitigates against coalitions between men and women, which I believe provide the only means for social change in our time. Political bonds need to be formed among female and male feminists and pro-feminists, people of color, gays and lesbians, as well as those disenfranchised by virtue of their class.

While scholarship within art practice and the museum profession (which is part of it) has paralleled the stages that Banner delineates, there are a few compelling differences as well. It seems, as she suggests, that as we are advancing we are rejecting the first and second stages of documenting discrimination and identifying female traditions in favor of the more theoretical and analytical stage three. For example, new and compelling debates about essentialism have emerged.[1] To women of color, for whom identity is a critical issue, the concept of a basic female identity may be a necessary tool for reclaiming the self. We do not all have the same histories, ideologies, or concerns. And calling for the end of the canon, which is central to stage three, is also problematic. As several of my black, Asian, and Hispanic colleagues point out, some of us are interested in dismantling the canon at the very moment when artists of color are about to enter it. This most recent stage has, finally, created an ironic reversal in the feminism of the late sixties and early seventies, which was disposed to practice rather than to theory. Today feminism faces the danger of becoming all theory and no practice. I agree wholeheartedly with Banner that one of the major contributions women can make is the creation of nonhierarchical, interactive models. This would involve what such feminists as Jane Gallop, Julia Kristeva, and Gayatri Spivak have called for in their analyses of power and authority. According to Gallop, "One can effectively undo authority only from the position of authority, in a way that exposes the illusion of that position without renouncing it."[2]

So far, it is only women who are interested in this strategy, and in the museum field such a concept is virtually unheard of. The museum that I direct has been evolving a management model over many years based on transparency— shared knowledge and decision making, self-criticism, and collaboration. For many reasons, among the forty-two people on staff, this process is extremely difficult and complex, albeit enormously rewarding. It will continue to evolve and to change for as long as the museum exists, perhaps using as models the precedents for consensual management such as women's self-help collectives, community action groups, alternative schools and day-care programs, and neighborhood-building initiatives.

This is a time not only to acknowledge and respect our differences but also to find commonalities across gender, race, and class positions. I believe that this will occur if we agree that our primary goal as feminists is first and foremost to effect real social change in the existing political and cultural structures.

NOTES

1. For the debate on essentialism, see *Differences: A Journal of Feminist Cultural Studies* 1 (Summer 1989). The theme of this issue is "The Essential Difference: Another Look at Essentialism."

2. See Jane Gallop, *Reading Lacan* (Ithaca, N.Y.: Cornell University Press, 1985).

PART 3

The Impact of Feminist Scholarship in Collections, Exhibitions, and Publications

IF FEMINIST scholarship is having an impact in museums, has there also been significant, substantive, and balanced gender representation in collections, exhibitions, and publications? Are there responsible and ethical attitudes in museums today? Also, where does museum leadership stand on gender issues? These questions are very important yet very broad.

There is a tendency to confuse two issues. One concerns the number of women belonging to a particular field, whether in academia or the museum world; and the other involves the articulation and representation of a feminist perspective that informs exhibitions and other presentations and that, presumably, even men are capable of providing. (There is not a lot of evidence for that, but there is hope.) It is important to register the numbers of women in the field. This, however, does not automatically demonstrate a feminist perspective, if achieving the recasting of museums, exhibitions, departments, and disciplines is the goal.

I wonder how in successful exhibitions the feminist perspective has been best employed. I suggest that one strategy might be to actively attempt feminist criticism of exhibitions that already exist. A gender equity group has been organized at the National Museum of American History to critique all existing exhibitions from a feminist perspective. We are beginning to see formal reviews of exhibitions in journals. If we review what is being done already and evaluate it from a feminist perspective, we would begin to shape the wider discussion of what constitutes success for diversity of perspective in museum presentations. That, to me, would be a start.

Marc Pachter

New Angles of Vision

Edith P. Mayo

I HAVE chosen to examine how the new feminist scholarship has been incorporated into exhibitions, not only because they are the most visible manifestation of its impact, but also because it would be exceedingly difficult to assess changes in museums without an extensive survey of exhibitions. I address the concept of "women's history as empowerment" and make an impassioned appeal that we create the climate and the support mechanisms needed to foster meaningful women's history in the public arena. At present we may have greater numbers of exhibitions by and about women, which is quite different from exhibitions that incorporate the new scholarship on women.

Here are a few examples of the current status of exhibitions or historic sites about women. Several years ago there was an exhibition in the Museum of the City of New York entitled "Beyond the Golden Door," which concerned New York's settlement house movement and the settlements' work with immigrants and the poor. It was a wonderful show but provided no indication of the impact of women, who largely ran the settlements, nor of the use of the term "settlement house." The choice of that term was not accidental. The women who founded settlement houses were deliberately using a politicized domestic space, one that intentionally brought the domestic ethic into public life.

Other exhibitions that have been considered "women's topics"—primarily those dealing with period costume—lacked a women's history framework. Two examples are: "The Proper Lady: Fashion and Etiquette in the 1880s," a costume exhibition at the Chicago Historical Society; and "Dressed for Work," a costume exhibit in the Valentine Museum in Richmond, Virginia, which had a lengthy accompanying essay placing the costumes on display more in a labor history than women's history framework. My assessment was that an average visitor would not have perceived a women's history framework from viewing the exhibition itself. Both of the exhibitions were presented essentially as costume shows. "Twenty-five Years of Barbie," an exhibition at the Indiana State Museum, might have been nostalgia, corporate advertising, or even a history of childhood and play, but women's history it was not.

By contrast, other exhibitions *have* shown the impact of the new women's history scholarship. Examples include "First Person Singular," a special exhibition on Eleanor Roosevelt at the National Museum of American History on the centennial of her birth; "Dress for Greater Freedom," a costume exhibition organized by the Oakland Museum in the early seventies, which traced women's changing roles and status through changes in dress; and "Men and Women: A History of Costume, Gender and Power" at the National Museum of American History.

Few national historic sites reflect the impact of the new feminist scholarship. Of the hundreds of National Park Service sites in this country, only six commemorate women: Eleanor Roosevelt's "Val Kil," the Clara Barton National Historic Site, the Mary McLeod Bethune House, the Sewall-Belmont House (headquarters of the National Woman's Party), the Maggie Walker site in Richmond, Virginia, and the Woman's Rights National Historic Park in Seneca Falls, New York. The National Historic and National Landmark Programs designate sites that have exceptional value for illustrating or interpreting the nation's history. Despite the fact that these programs of the U.S. Department of the Interior are more than twenty-five years old, less than 5 percent of the approximately two thousand historic sites focus on women.

In 1989 the Women's History Landmarks Study was begun with the support of the National Park Service, the Organization of American Historians, and the National Coordinating Committee for the Promotion of History. The study identified sites that reflect the women's history framework, considerations of class, race, and ethnicity, as well as women's contributions to labor, education, reform, and politics. Seven scholars in women's history with expertise in specific areas were commissioned to prepare broad thematic essays, incorporating both the most recent scholarship in women's history and knowledge of historic sites associated with women's experiences and contributions in order to establish contexts for site selections. Despite this extensive scholarly input, the Women's History Landmarks coordinator, Page Miller (director of the National Coordinating Committee for the Promotion of History), confided at a Washington Women Historians' meeting that the project had met with resistance over sites, and that the list of sites in general had been characterized as "the three L's—leftist, labor, and lesbian." Although some forty sites were initially submitted, in 1990 only twenty-four were under consideration for landmark designation.

Scholarly literature on women's history in museums and other public history venues is still a rather scarce phenomenon. Barbara Melosh of the National Museum of American History and I have both written articles on the presentation of women's history exhibitions in museums, as has Barbara Howe of West Virginia University and the National Council on Public History.[1]

I am certain that most people know how history is written. It is not "just the facts, ma'am" but a deliberate construction. It consists of an interpretation of the facts that is structured with a particular viewpoint or bias by a particular group or groups and looks at the past to understand, to give meaning to, or to justify the present. Major work in the field is currently concerned with how history is constructed. The collection of essays in *Presenting the Past: Essays on History and the Public*, by Barbara Melosh and Christina Simmons, uncovers the construction of history in many well-known historic sites, popular history journals, and mass-media "historic" presentations. Three important scholarly articles about the construction of historical memory are Michael Frisch's "The Memory of History" and Michael Wallace's "Reflections on the History of Historic Preservation" and "The Future of History Museums."[2]

As an example of how history is constructed, and of the political or social viewpoints it can represent, we should look at the struggle being waged over the interpretation of the Vietnam War among those on the right, left, and center for the hearts and minds of the students who read textbooks and watch educational films. Since history is a construction, I would suggest that whoever controls the interpretation of the past controls the politics and economics of the present. Women must understand this, if they want to see their history in museums.

A number of factors work against the incorporation of feminist scholarship in museum exhibitions. One is that women are not often perceived as a legitimate constituency by museum administrators, by funders, and often by women themselves. Women's exhibits are considered legitimate if they present traditional "women's" topics such as costume, quilting, or decorative arts, or if women are depicted as leading "attendant" lives—that is, attached to some other cultural or historical group such as African Americans, Native Americans, or presidents. Another factor is that as exhibition money from the public sector continues to dwindle, corporations by their funding trends often determine what the public sees as history in museums. Also, women themselves and the funding agencies that support women's activist policies do not view history as empowerment. While many individual women and funding foundations will support "activist politics" or "activist policies" for women, they do not perceive the direct correlation between the historical visibility of women and its relationship to power, economics, and the equalization of gender in the present.

Other groups do not miss this connection. For example, look at the development of the National Museum of the American Indian and the possible Smithsonian Institution–sponsored African American museum, as well as the celebration of Black History month. During Black History Month, newspapers, schools, museums, television, and other media acknowledge the achievements of African Americans in a wise move to recognize and to support the group's legitimacy. Black History Month was even celebrated in the American History Museum's cafeteria! It was a delight to see such recognition; however, when I asked whether the food vendor was planning activities for Women's History Month, I received an uncomprehending stare. "What's that?" was the response.

Because both women themselves and funding agencies fail to perceive the connection between women's visibility in history and empowerment, it is extremely difficult to fund meaningful women's history exhibitions. Or perhaps funders do see the connection but do not wish to support such legitimacy for women. Perhaps women's history is still perceived as trivial and not "real history."

Within the National Museum of American History, exhibitions with a women's history framework have experienced difficulty in raising funds. These exhibitions have included "Men and Women: A History of Costume, Gender, and Power," which was finally supported by a generous grant from the Cosmetology Institute, as well as by the Smithsonian Institution's Special Exhibition Fund; "From Parlor to Politics: Women and Reform in America," which was also ultimately supported by the Institution's Special Exhibition Fund; and the reinterpretation and reinstallation of the First Ladies Hall. Funders must begin to view women's visibility in history as empowerment, and women must make them understand this connection. Without that understanding, we may continue to see more exhibitions on women but not see those that are grounded in women's history.

Other factors also work against the incorporation of feminist scholarship in the public sector. First is the tendency among younger women historians, understandably intent on proving their own scholarly viability, to undermine or to detract from the women professionals who preceded them. They should understand, having studied the systematic, pervasive disadvantaging of women and the unfolding of women's life patterns prior to the second women's movement, why women who are now in the middle years of their lives lack Ph.D.s and other credentials. It has nothing to do with brainpower and everything to do with discrimination. This undermining of predecessors is destructive to the collegial atmosphere among women in the museum profession and makes women themselves complicit in the continuing reinforcement of sexist structures existing both within the museum field and society.

Another factor is that museum administrators have not developed a serious commitment to the support and the underwriting of feminist scholarship in museums and other public history arenas, including research time, publication venues, adequate monetary support, and defense of possibly controversial positions.

Finally, it is not yet widely recognized that women's history is more than simply factoring women into existing, traditional models developed for and by men. We have considered history primarily in male-defined terms rather than from a female-centered value system. We have asked questions of history inappropriate to women's experiences. Filtered through the prism of gender, history can be modified, providing a different angle of vision that brings an altered perspective on the world.

Not until the theories and methodologies by which we research, write, and understand history are defined by women as well as by men; not until the constructions by which history is created and written become angles of vision held by women and not by men; not until the questions we ask of history are defined also by women; and not until the breakdown of historical periods reflects the patterns of women's lives and women's consciousness will we see meaningful women's history in museums. The impact of the new scholarship on women will not emerge until these conditions are met and until women themselves claim their heritage and demand to see their own history.

NOTES

1. Barbara Melosh and Christina Simmons, "Exhibiting Women's History," in *Presenting the Past: Essays on History and the Public,* ed. Susan Porter Benson, Stephen

Brier, and Roy Rozenzweig (Philadelphia: Temple University Press, 1986), 203–21; Edith P. Mayo, "A New View?" *Museum News* 69 (July–August 1990): 48–50; and Barbara J. Howe and Emory L. Kemps, eds., *Public History: An Introduction* (Malabar, Fla.: Robert E. Krieger Publishing, 1986).

2. Michael H. Frisch, "The Memory of History," in *Presenting the Past*, ed. Benson et al., 5–17; Michael Wallace, "Reflections on the History of Historic Preservation," in *Presenting the Past*, ed. Benson et al., 165–99; and Michael Wallace, "The Future of History Museums," *History News* 44 (July–August 1989): 5–8, 30–33.

Attitudes toward Gender Equity

Esin Atil

MY COMMENTS are restricted to my area of specialization, Islamic art and civilization. I concentrate on two issues in the Islamic world: women who are directors or departmental heads in national museums, and exhibitions and publications devoted to women artists. It may be surprising that there are more women heading cultural organizations and museums in Islamic countries than in Europe and the United States combined. This is a high imbalance, considering that there are relatively few public museums in the Islamic world compared to hundreds in Europe and the United States. For over ten years a woman has been the Minister of Culture in Syria. Women are or have been directors of internationally known collections in Iran, Kuwait, Bahrain, Yemen, Turkey, Egypt, and Tunisia. Most of these women are scholars—art historians or archaeologists—although a few may have begun their careers in administration or education. There are many more women heading departments, including curatorial, conservation, and archival research departments. At international conferences these scholars present some of the most outstanding and provocative papers, frequently outshining the men from their countries.

Has this significant intellectual force made a major contribution to feminist scholarship in my field? Not really. These women are overwhelmed by the vast amount of items deposited in their museums, some collected for centuries by royal or princely courts, others unearthed each season during archaeological excavations. While the majority of objects in American museums have been individually selected and researched before acquisition, those in the Islamic world were literally dumped by the thousands into national museums, many of which were founded when these countries became independent states after World War I. The concerns of women in these museums are far more fundamental than ours. They are interested in taking inventory of the collections, documenting each item, preparing exhibitions and catalogs, and lastly—if time allows—pursuing their scholarly research and publications. This they accomplish despite financial restrictions (the only exceptions are in one or two wealthy Arabian Gulf States) and unbelievably bureaucratic red tape. Although the concept of feminist scholarship is absent, what does exist is scholarship by women. Much the same situation occurs in the academic world, in which the primary concern of women provosts, deans, department heads, and professors is to be esteemed scholars, regardless of their sex. In fact, they stress an asexual intellectualism. Their mothers and grandmothers fought sexual discrimination for centuries, and now these modern women want equal recognition for achievements.

It may be surprising too that there are exhibitions and publications devoted to Islamic women artists, and a number of societies for women artists throughout the Islamic world, from Indonesia to Morocco. These societies include women weavers, painters, sculptors, potters, and metalworkers, as well as architects, interior decorators, and fashion or textile designers, who periodically assemble exhibitions and circulate them. This type of gender separatism in exhibitions might be frowned upon by some of the local liberals, but it works superbly and is ideally suited for Islamic societies. Even Saudi Arabia has become active in such exhibitions devoted to women artists.

Historical studies on women in the arts do not yet exist, and in my opinion, cannot exist since Islamic artists traditionally did not feel obliged to inscribe their names on their works. Consequently, there are few signed and dated objects through some fifteen hundred years of Islamic art. Although there have been biographies of artists, only a small percentage of the names listed in them can be identified with existing pieces, none of which were made by women. A number of women are mentioned as being poets and writers, but mostly in the later periods—that is, in the nineteenth and twentieth centuries.

Something fascinating has recently developed: patronage by women in Islamic art and architecture. Throughout the history of Islamic civilization, women have been highly instrumental in sponsoring architectural complexes that included religious, charitable, social, and educational institutions. They also endowed them with objects, furnishings, and funds that supplied salaries and supported activities and maintenance. These patrons, of course, belonged to the upper classes. A few were rulers in their own right and many more were wives and daughters of sultans or affluent princes. One of the most remarkable women was Hurrem, the wife of the sixteenth-century Turkish sultan Suleiman the Magnificent. She was the first to hire the great architect Sinan, who built for her a complex that included a mosque, a school, a soup kitchen, an alms house, and a hospital for women—the earliest women's hospital in history. Although the original building has been destroyed, on its site today is Istanbul's modern hospital for women, which is named for Hurrem.

I chose the theme of patronage for my exhibition on Islamic art on loan from Kuwait. I specifically asked the contributors to the catalog to highlight the role of women. Some remarkable personages evolved, and their legacy has continued for hundreds of years.

While exhibitions and publications on living and past women artists are important to understand artistic traditions, aesthetics, and cultural changes that occur or have occurred, historical studies should not neglect the importance of women as patrons—sponsors of art, collectors, and trendsetters.

The time will come when women scholars in the Islamic world, in both curatorial and academic fields, will feel confident in having attained equality with the opposite sex and will then concentrate on the contributions of their gender to civilization. Hopefully what has already begun is the first chapter of what Edith P. Mayo calls in her essay, "New Angles of Vision," "history as empowerment."

Balancing Gender Representation

Frank Talbot

WOMEN HAVE played an extremely strong role at the highest levels of scholarship, exhibitions, and administration in natural history museums. They have also affected all aspects of museums' operations.

In the Australian Museum, in which I worked from 1964 to 1975, all early curators other than the director had no degrees. Its first curator with a degree was Elizabeth Pope, a marine scientist. When I became the museum's director, she was the obvious choice for a deputy director.

I then moved to the California Academy of Sciences, where historically the most significant curatorial figure was Alice Eastwood. She was known for literally having run, leaving behind her own house, to the Academy after the 1906 earthquake in order to save most of the topical collections, important books, and all the museum's registers from a fire that swept down Market Street and ultimately destroyed the Academy's original building. She is the only curator in the 147-year history of the Academy whose story is celebrated in a display hall, providing an exceptional role model for young people.

One also cannot help but mention that amazing scholar, Margaret Mead. Friends of mine who worked at the American Museum of Natural History in New York and had not seen Mead came to the conclusion that she was not one person but "a committee on the fifth floor."

When I was very young, twenty-two years old, I went to Britain to begin my first job at the University of Durham. I had a brand-new master's degree, and as a taxonomist I frequently visited and worked in the British Museum. Many of the prestigious people in the field at that time were women such as Marie Lebour and Sydney Manton (a Fellow of the Royal Society, the highest accolade that can be given to anyone in Britain in the scientific field), as well as British Museum scientists Isabella Gordon, Ethylwyn Trewavas, and Rosemary Lowe.

In the National Museum of Natural History there have been some powerful women curators such as Mary Rathburn in the Crustacea Department and Betty Meggers in the Anthropology Department, as well as many young curators who are extremely important in the museum, because they shape its exhibitions and intellectual output. I am delighted to say that the Museum of Natural History's executive committee now consists of three men and four women.

Let me examine employment searches for women academics in museums, because this is an extremely important area. There has, of course, been discrimination in the past. Over the last thirty years, in four museums and one university, I have been involved in numerous employment searches, and there undoubtedly was no gender bias in our choices. We fought bitterly over issues, approaches, and scholarship, but gender was irrelevant. We chose women as postdoctoral researchers, assistants, associates, and full curators. We also selected them for positions at the university at all levels to full chairs, including a deanship.

There remains much bad news. There is still a preponderance of men in curatorial positions. Why is this so? If you look at the people who are now entering the field and who respond to our advertisements, there is still a great majority of men in the applicant pool for scholarly positions, partially because few women have chosen to take this path. That in itself may be due to educational biases. Some disciplines such as anthropology and botany have had more women than others. In fields such as the paleontological and mineral sciences, however, there is a dearth of women, perhaps because there have been few role models and women have not been encouraged to enter those fields. In one natural science museum, for example, the great figures in atomic physics hang on a wall in the hall. You would expect that Marie Curie would have her rightful place there, but she does not. Her husband Pierre is figured prominently in front, and she is looking over his shoulder. Clearly, in the past males dominated this museum. It is interesting to note that for the last few years this primary physics museum has been run by an outstanding woman director.

In the next few decades there will be a shortage of some half a million science and engineering graduates. Also, many more women and minorities will be entering the work force. An increase in the number of women and minorities will occur in the sciences only if we attract them to the field, and at present I do not think we are doing so. Sparking the imagination of young minds, providing the appropriate history of exemplary women scientists in our display areas, deliberately seeking female interns at the undergraduate level, and providing scholarships for graduate work will all be necessary to attract more women to the field and to redress what is clearly a long-standing wrong. We can do a lot about the gender imbalance in the scholastic area, although we have done very little. We have not really encouraged women, and it is clear that even now we have not given them their rightful place in history.

I do not feel, however, that most natural history museums are creating heavily male-dominated scholarship or exhibitions today. Most of them include young scholars with a feminist viewpoint. A good balance of female scholars and leaders in exhibitions, education, and administration would help us diversify even more.

PART 4

Contemporary Initiatives in Ethnic Museums, Children's Museums, and Science and Technology Centers

THE ASSOCIATION of Science and Technology Centers (ASTC), a professional organization of 326 science museums in the United States and abroad, was founded in 1971 by the directors of sixteen leading science and technology centers. Dixie Lee Ray, director of the Pacific Science Center in Seattle, was the only woman among the organization's founders. Some eighteen years later the ASTC membership elected its first woman president of the board, Freda Nicholson, the executive director of the Science Museums of Charlotte, North Carolina. I regret that it took so long!

The ASTC has been challenged to expand the participation of minorities, people with disabilities, and women through the Community Group Partnership Program, a three-year effort supported by the Carnegie Corporation of New York. The organization plans to take a practical look at gender perspectives as they influence the operations and the activities of ethnic museums, children's museums, and science and technology centers, which all have historical roots, although the majority of them are relatively young. Most of them, however, have experienced their greatest growth in numbers and in size during the sixties and seventies, coinciding with the women's movement. Central to the mission of these museums is to convey culture and to educate youth, which the preceding essays have described as the traditional nurturing roles of women in many cultures. Ethnic museums, children's museums, and science and technology centers are also populist institutions. Many of them seek to respond to the needs of their local communities as a means to project that bigger picture, which Mary Schmidt Campbell describes in the introduction. As much as funding and resources allow, these institutions are also committed to experimentation with creative and sometimes ambitious approaches to involve girls and women of diverse classes, races, and cultures.

Bonnie VanDorn

The Empowerment of African American Museums

Rowena Stewart

IT IS probably impossible to ascertain who founded the first black museum. Certainly some of the leaders of the African American Museums Association must be recognized as pioneers of the black museum movement. They include Margaret Burroughs, founder of the DuSable Museum of African American History in Chicago; Edmund B. Gaither, director of the National Center for Afro-American Artists in Boston; Charles Wright, founder of the Museum of African American History in Detroit; Mary Schmidt Campbell, the first director of the Studio Museum in Harlem and currently dean of the Tisch School of the Arts in New York; Byron Rushing, formerly the director of the African Meeting House in Boston and currently state representative for Massachusetts; and the late John Kinard, formerly the director of the Smithsonian Institution's Anacostia Museum.

Each of these directors had a unique perspective, yet they all shared a common goal and understanding. They were guided by their dedication to telling the truth about the African American struggle in America, as well as by their realization that traditional museums were established under a discriminatory system and did not serve the needs of the African American community.

At the same time it was clear that the museum movement, as it existed in the larger traditional society, was a legitimate and a potentially successful means to visualize the culture of people of African descent. After all, the earlier traditional museums had helped to convince most Americans that white Anglo-Saxon Protestants made up this country, when in actuality the nation was made up of slaves, free men and women, indentured people of all races, and men and women of various ethnic groups. The very fact that the American museum movement is now over eight thousand strong since its birth in the eighteenth century is proof that cultural institutions which provide positive images, even at the expense of other groups, can have a definite and major influence on the education of its people.

Early black museum leaders also realized that traditional museums served to visually reinforce the concept of a white America. Minutes after entering the average museum, one is aware that it constitutes an image of America. This explains, at least partially, why Americans who see no reflections of themselves in such museums rarely patronize them. "Field to Factory"—the first major exhibition on the African American experience produced by the National Museum of American History at the Smithsonian Institution—however, attracted a record number of African American visitors.

It was obvious to the early founders of the black museum movement that traditional museums usually depicted blacks as subservient to whites. Many exhibits had displayed only negative portrayals, although it was widely known in the African American community that both positive and negative African American images and artifacts were in the collections of major museums.

Exhibitions were first held in the twenties at early expositions on Negro History Day, which evolved into Black History Month in 1976. During the civil rights movement artists used their work to arouse social, cultural, and historical concerns. Their works were heroic and dramatic, containing narratives that expressed the aspirations and the dreams of their people. Black museums also emerged from this need to express pride in the African American heritage and to assert its roots. These museums have been mandated to educate and to interpret African American culture to the community at large. The founders of black museums recognized the power of their institutions and sought to document the experiences of people of African descent, using the museums to tell the remarkable story of their survival in a new land. This was to be the story of a people who had come to this country, the majority as slaves, yet managed over time to struggle, to survive, and to make positive contributions to American society.

The search for truth in African American history was probably first launched by Carter G. Woodson, who founded the Association for the Study of Negro Life and History in 1915. Slowly and methodically, he encouraged scholars to research, to write, and to publish in the area of black history. He also challenged the published history, becoming in the process the "keeper of the record" of the African American struggle. More importantly, under Woodson's guidance, the Association for the Study of Negro Life and History began and continues to hold annual black history programs that celebrate the survival of African American people. His organization was supported by average citizens who believed that understanding African American culture was important, and who met annually to learn about the latest research on black history and culture. Their children frequently attended historically black colleges and would often return to the community churches and organizations to discuss issues that had been uncovered about their own history.

Early African American institutions realized the value of museums. During the Civil War and immediately following it, schools and colleges were established to educate the newly emancipated African American citizens. Penn Center on Saint Helena Island, South Carolina, Fisk University in Nashville, and Hampton Institute in Hampton, Virginia, were among the earliest schools to be founded for this purpose. Their archives, as well as those of other African American Institutions, are rich in records of past struggles and contributions, although their collections have been and continue to be seriously neglected. Efforts to maintain such archives have been aided by the scholarly research of librarians, like Dorothy Porter Wesley of the Mooreland Springarn Collection and Jean Hutson of the Schomburg Center for Research in Black Culture, who have constantly uncovered new information. Both the Mooreland Springarn Collection and the Schomburg Center for Research in Black Culture contain extensive collections and remain among the principal sources of information on the African American experience.

The founders of the black museum movement sought to visualize the experience of their people by borrowing from European technology, while continuing to respect the oral tradition of Africa. The oral tradition is not only an important element in African American history and culture but also is often the principal repository of black history. The vitality of the oral tradition is exemplified by the eighteenth-century "Election Day" ceremonies. These events, which took place before the American Revolution, were community rituals in which slaves celebrated the holiday by electing mock officials to govern themselves. The celebrations included telling stories about the African past. Similarly, in the nineteenth and twentieth centuries oral history has been formally transmitted at Emancipation Day celebrations—observances that began soon after 1838 to acknowledge the manumission of slaves in the West Indies. These annual celebrations also became rituals in certain African American communities such as Saint Helena Island, South Carolina, and Providence, Rhode Island.

In *Music of Black Americans,* Eileen Southern observes that major historically black colleges, such as Fisk University and Hampton Institute, introduced the music of slaves as public performances in 1867. In 1871, as a means of raising money to support higher education for blacks, the Fisk Jubilee Singers began to perform publicly throughout the country, often for audiences that had never heard African American folk music. They also performed before royalty in Europe and commoners in Germany, Switzerland, and Great Britain. The Fisk singers took their audiences by storm and won widespread critical acclaim. In concerts they visualized an experience through the oral tradition that had preserved the folk songs of the past, performing a spiritual representation of plantation songs.[1]

Women in the African American museum movement participated in the search for truth, perceiving that their responsibility as descendants of African society was to nurture, to educate, and to maintain the family genealogies, rituals, and traditions. Their ancestors had arrived in America—some free and some enslaved—with an understanding of how these rituals and traditions could provide hope in desperate times. The women were guardians of the African symbolic estate, which Barry Gaither describes as "a political and artistic place for all black people on the stage of world history."[2]

Much is unknown about African women before the influence of Islam and Christianity, but there is enough scholarly information from the written records after the arrival of the conquerors to indicate the enduring power of their cultural integrity. For example, when a religion was forced upon the Africans, they often created secret religious orders designed for emancipation, which were transplanted to America in the form of "benevolent societies" during the eighteenth and nineteenth centuries. Women's benevolent societies were active in establishing schools, holding celebrations, fostering creative art, music, and literature, and promoting an understanding of Africa and its people. Women of the African Benevolent Society, for example, observed a "Day of Humiliation" to protest the conditions blacks were enduring in this country "as poor despised Africans in this foreign land." The women raised money but allowed the men in the organization to assume the leadership role.

In the twentieth century African American women have continued the search for truth, but in a more visible institution—the black museum. They had come to terms with being African and American and, adopting the strategy of the dominant culture, used the museum, which was a very powerful institution in American culture, to pursue their agenda. Like their ancestors had, black women in this century brought passion, nurturing, and clear goals to their efforts to educate and to pass on the rituals of the past.

The civil rights movement of the sixties made it possible for Americans to view people of African descent differently and, most importantly, to reject the history established by the dominant culture. This revolutionary movement was not only for the intellectuals but for the public, whose cries were for "a place to tell my story and select my hero," as well as "a place for history and art in my neighborhood."[3] These feelings and demands instilled in the African American home were based on the recognition that "there are more heroes in our culture than Booker T. Washington, Harriet Tubman, Richard Allen, and George Washington Carver."[4]

Black neighborhoods now proclaimed ownership of their history, and suddenly art and history appeared on the sides of buildings. Using the technique of Mexican muralist Diego Rivera, people and artists together proclaimed their truth and their art in what is called the "contemporary mural movement." Black women nurtured, educated, witnessed, and participated in this mural movement. It was in this environment that the African American museum came into being. Margaret Burroughs and Charles Wright began the black museum movement with special emphasis on fostering the founding of African American museums.

Women of the twentieth-century African American museum movement can be categorized as founder/activist, scholar/museum professional, those who struggled for African American representation in the nonblack institutions in which they worked, and patrons of the arts. The founder/activist was a woman who actively participated in the civil or human rights movements and sought to establish a museum because she believed in empowerment through history and culture. She also had a clear understanding of the politics of art and history. Examples of founder/activists were Margaret Burroughs, organizer of the DuSable Museum of African American History in Chicago, artist, poet, and political activist, and Elma Lewis, founder of the National Center of Afro-American Art in Boston. Noted black historic preservationist Joan Maynard can also be seen as a founder/activist. Maynard worked as a graphic artist for an early National Association for the Advancement of Colored People (NAACP) publication and is currently restoring Weeksville, a nineteenth-century free-black community in Brooklyn, of which four buildings have survived. She hopes that it will become a place of hope for residents of the public housing project that adjoins the site.

The scholar/museum professionals were not founders of institutions but rather initiators of a major effort to stabilize the museum movement. Leading this effort was Mary Schmidt Campbell, who reorganized and stabilized the Studio Museum in Harlem, which became the first accredited black museum.

Sylvia Williams, director of the National Museum of African Art, played a major part in the museum's development, transforming a dream into reality at the Smithsonian Institution.

The third category is women who are not working in black museums but in other major museums, where they are fighting for African American representation in the dominant culture. This group includes Cheryl McClenney Brooker, deputy director of the Philadelphia Museum of Art, and Lowery Sims, associate curator of twentieth-century art at the Metropolitan Museum of Art in New York.

Another category includes black women whose families have cultivated and nurtured their love for the arts. Black women patrons of the arts and prestigious social organizations such as the Links and Delta Sigma Theta Sorority, which support and foster knowledge of the arts, are also represented in this category. Americans cannot forget the February 1978 opening of the "Afro-American Tradition in Decorative Art," an exhibition at the Cleveland Museum of Art that was sponsored by the Links, black women with an affinity for art. In some instances, these women have become founders of museums and heads of organizations. They include women such as Aurelia Brooks of the California Museum of Afro-American History and Culture, and organizations such as the Mary McLeod Bethune Museum and Archives, which is gathering documentation on the black women's club movement.

In general, women in museums have too often remained silent while their institutions have moved forward. In the twenty-first century African American women must take more responsibility for telling the whole story of their struggles and contributions. They have been guardians but can no longer remain invisible. They too are the keepers of the African estate.

NOTES

1. See Eileen Southern, *The Music of Black Americans: A History* (New York: W. W. Norton, 1971).

2. Edmund B. Gaither, "Politics and the African Legacy," in *Ethnicity Art and Politics; and Exploration* (Providence: Rhode Island Black Studies Consortium, 1983), 7–10.

3. See *The People's Art: Black Murals, 1967–1978* (Philadelphia: Afro-American Historical and Cultural Museum, 1986).

4. Ibid.

Empowering the Mind of the Child in Children's Museums

Ann W. Lewin

I WISH I could say that children's museums are as united in their agenda as African American museums. There is, however, a debate among children's museums about their mission: Should we collect—because, after all, we are museums—or should our hallmark be learning by doing? I speak strongly for my own museum, whose mission is not collecting but empowering the mind of the child. Since there is a child in all of us, I see children's museums as places for fostering lifelong learning for everyone.

It is said that it takes fifty years for any new theory of education to enter the classroom. Children's museums, however, can decrease the gap between theory and practice. In these museums new research on cognitive ability can reach the public so that it can be used and tested. The new theories are dynamic. For example, Reuven Feuerstein's theory of mediated learning builds on Jean Piaget's concept of learning by doing. Feuerstein believes that although individuals must have a basis in learning through experience, the experience must be mediated. Progressing from simply learning by doing to a mediated learning experience is one of the great challenges that faces children's museums in the next decade. Howard Gardner, codirector of Project Zero at the Harvard University Graduate School of Education, presents his theory of multiple intelligences in *Frames of Mind*. This theory is practiced in children's museums, in which children explore the kinesthetic, spatial, linguistic, mathematical, musical, interpersonal, and intrapersonal skills that constitute Gardner's "seven intelligences."[1] Lev Vigotsky has studied the environment's influence on learning. Children's museums are applying his theory in exhibitions that incorporate realistic settings and recreate a variety of social interactions. There is thus great potential in children's museums to bring theory into practice, and that is an important and challenging role.

The first children's museum was the Brooklyn Children's Museum, which opened in 1899 and was followed by the Boston Children's Museum in 1911. The birth of children's museums as we know them in today's interactive, hands-on-learning form, however, occurred in the mid-sixties, when Mike Spock at the Boston Children's Museum had the innovative vision of packing away the collections, throwing out the glass cases, and constructing large-scale interactive props to facilitate children's learning. Albert Heine at the Corpus Christi Children's Museum in Corpus Christi, Texas, was among the first to mount interactive exhibits. Frank Oppenheimer founded the San Francisco Exploratorium as a science museum, but it became a primary force in the development of hands-on learning in museums. The Ontario Science Center, born at about the same time as the Exploratorium, had a large staff that similarly pioneered interactive exhibits. Lloyd Hezakiah, as director of the Brooklyn Children's Museum, changed its focus from collections to hands-on learning orientation. Jane R. Glaser, as head of the Children's Museum and Planetarium (now the Sunrise Museum) in Charleston, West Virginia, created a highly interactive and experiential program. Doris Whitmore, at the Children's Museum (now the Jacksonville Museum of Science and History) in Jacksonville, Florida, achieved wonderful results with total environments as the basis for learning, and Mildred S. Compton at the Indianapolis Children's Museum pioneered after-school activities. In short, there were about seven pioneers in the children's museum field, among whom three women figure prominently. These people began their work from the early sixties to the seventies. In the eighties the number of children's museums in America grew to at least three hundred.

Women's roles in the founding and the development of children's museums have been enormous. An estimated 85 to 95 percent of the founders, the directors, and the activists in children's museums are women. The impetus for the establishment of these museums has frequently come from the Junior League, a venerable women's organization in towns and cities across the country. (Interestingly, the former director of the Association of Youth Museums, Linda Eidiken, has observed, the vast majority of the founders and directors of children's museums who are practicing in the field now either have no children or have grown children. They do not have infants, toddlers, or small children.)

As the prime movers in the children's museum movement, women have played every conceivable role. They have founded museums, performed all the initial organizational tasks, raised the money, created the programs, handled the public relations, and directed the institutions. Their initiative has led to the development of many new institutions across the country.

I do not see a gender bias in children's museums. Their mission is to empower the mind. They are not historical and do not reflect where we have come as a society. They instead focus on: How do I think? How do I make this work? What interaction is going to take place between me and these exhibits?

Children's museums can be seen as a driving force in the museum field for examining issues relevant to underclass or minority populations. Multiculturalism, as well as women's impact on museums, can be viewed from four different stances: content of exhibits, interpretation of exhibits, audience, and staff. In terms of content, children's museums consciously reach out to new audiences, many feeling a strong sense of social responsibility to do so. Children's museums also believe that it is important for the content of the material they present to be socially relevant and are thus conscious of reflecting minority views in their exhibitions. Children's museums have offered some major exhibits on African Americans and several on Native Americans, as well as an exhibit on the population of rural Appalachia. There has not yet been an exhibit that focuses specifically on differences between the genders. It would be interesting to see how a children's museum exhibit would present this issue.

In terms of interpretation of an exhibit's content, there is a growing trend in children's museums to emphasize feelings. This is grounded in the theoretical work of the psychologist Mihaly Csikszentmihalyi, head of the Department of Behavioral Sciences at the University of Chicago. He argues that although educators have focused for decades on learning content, it is irrelevant if the students are not intrinsically motivated. Researchers studying motivation say that people are more likely to be motivated to learn if there is some emotive or feeling content associated with what they are learning. Examples of exhibits with emotional content include "What if I Couldn't," originated by the Boston Children's Museum, which examined feelings of people with disabilities; the Capital Children's Museum's very emotional exhibit, "Remember the Children," which used the Holocaust as a vehicle to explore prejudice and people's feelings and actions toward each other; and exhibits at the Teen Center at the Indianapolis Children's Museum, which have examined emotion-laden issues such as attitudes toward substance abuse and the prevention of early pregnancy. I predict that one of the children's museums will create an exhibit on what it feels like to be a girl, but I certainly hope they also do one on what it feels like to be a boy. A major challenge in interpreting any of these sensitive areas is to explode the cultural "shoulds"—what a girl "should" do and what a boy "should" do. This can be a challenge in part because museums too often reinforce rather than remove stereotypes, a problem that derives from an exhibit's having to compress so much information.

Who is the audience for children's museums? Sociological studies indicate that people of comfortable economic levels are most likely to expose their children to enriching experiences. For people of low economic levels, the struggle for subsistence makes it less likely that they will do so. Attendance at museums in Washington, D.C., supports this finding. The Capital Children's Museum is located in a transitional neighborhood in which the majority of the population is black, and has an unusually high representation of black visitors. That is not the case in virtually all of the other cultural institutions in this city. Location is a factor in who the audience is.

An examination of staffing in children's museums further reveals how museums reflect women's issues and women's impact on museums. Women dominate the staffs of children's museums. Why are there so many women leaders in the children's museum field, in which the main audience is children from ages two or three to nine or ten? Culturally, the fields of early childhood and primary education are almost entirely occupied by women, which is the legacy of the period when those were among the only jobs open to women. Our challenge is to encourage men to enter and to stay in the field.

Financial factors have also contributed to women dominating children's museum staffs. The education of children is undervalued in this country. A report by the Economic Policy Institute notes that

> United States public and private spending on pre-primary, primary, and secondary education is lower than in most other countries. Out of 16 industrial nations, we rank 14th in what we spend on children of those ages.[2]

A corporation, for example, may give one thousand dollars to the symphony and one hundred dollars to the children's museum. Such funding practices contribute to depressed salaries in children's museums.

Are girls being encouraged to enter the sciences and to study new technology through innovative museum programs at children's museums? Exhibits at children's museums do of course reflect science and new technology, although there has not been a broad-based movement to reach out specifically to girls in those exhibits. Studies show that in schools, boys rush into computer classes and literally elbow girls out of the way. This has not happened in children's museums, in which girls use computer exhibits as well as boys. One reason may be that children's museum staffs have so many women who provide on-site role models for the use of these exhibits. Girls are as likely to use pulleys and gears and computers as are boys.

The children's museum field is wide open to women, and women are decidedly leading the field. Moreover, the context of children's museums is not gender biased. Because gender does not present problems for women in children's museums, the more relevant issue is the museums' accessibility to minorities. This goes to the heart of an issue facing the entire nation: the challenge of addressing the problems of the underprivileged. What specifically can museums do about it?

NOTES

1. Howard Gardner, *Frames of Mind: The Theory of Multiple Intelligences* (New York: Basic Books, 1983).

2. "Shortchanging Education: How the U.S. Spending on Grades K through 12 Lags behind Other Industrial Nations," briefing paper, January 1990, Economic Policy Institute, Washington, D.C.

Bringing Civility to Science Museums

JoAllyn Archambault

WOMEN IN positions of authority have brought "civilization" to science museums. They have provided civility and a broader notion of cooperation and staff support than had previously existed. They have also initiated an intergenerational, interclass, and interracial dialogue that examines social realities and complexities that are as intricate and as interesting as subatomic physics. In the long history of science museums with a strong scholarly core, the curatorial atmosphere has been similar to that of the research university. Curators and staff are intensely focused on research, curatorial activities, academic publications, and producing exhibits that are based on research. Often, concentration on the scholarly work of the museum has been at the expense of the social dynamic of the workplace.

Female curators and museum administrators have made a difference in changing attitudes in the workplace, as have women in other professions. Management studies have documented that female administrators are more supportive of their staffs and take a more holistic attitude toward the workplace. Women are concerned for the entire institution and initiate activities and policies that are conducive to the health and productivity of the whole, not simply the individual. These management studies have been of private, profit-making businesses, but the same pattern can be observed in museums.

Women's behavior in the workplace stems from the social training that most women receive in this country, regardless of ethnicity or class. Women are taught to be socializers and nurturers. They continue to use their socializing and nurturing skills when they enter leadership positions. Women in museums have thus instituted a sociable atmosphere of staff interaction, which decreases the tendency toward isolation so common in research institutions and ultimately benefits the institutions.

Women have proven to be sensitive to the complexities of museum audiences in the same way they have been responsive to the social intricacies within their institutions. Female curators and administrators have been in the forefront of creating exhibits that are multilayered and address diverse audiences. They have helped to initiate a dialogue within the public interface that has both challenged and delighted new audiences. Exhibits of "boys and their toys" are no longer acceptable. Women have also assisted in the creation of installations dealing with the reality of social complexities, the universality of human experience, and the uniqueness of ethnic inheritance. They have created and supported exhibits that address the validity of non-Western societies, not draping them in exoticism or placing the peoples in a time warp but presenting them as citizens of the late twentieth century. Women have also dealt honestly with colonialism and political change and have not allowed the generic "native" to be a medium through which the dialogue takes place.

Women have been a formative influence in enlarging the public discourse, while recognizing the multiplicity of audience perspectives and messages. It has been neither an easy nor a widely recognized accomplishment. We should all congratulate women for their willingness and their ability to bring true civilization to museums and to their staffs, subject matter, and audiences.

Creating a Unified Effort

Zora Martin Felton

IN HER essay, "The Empowerment of African American Museums," Rowena Stewart has struck a number of sensitive chords. I agree with her statements about the search for truth in African American history and support her recognition that museums should be used as a mechanism to collect, to preserve, and to interpret the African American story.

From the small beginnings, there are now, according to the African American Museums Association, 120 African American museums. During the association's last survey, which was completed in 1987 and published in 1988, 42 percent of these were history museums and 15 percent were art museums. Eighty-nine percent were in urban areas, primarily in the East. The average staff had six people, and the number of visitors per year ranged from four hundred to two hundred thousand. Annual budgets varied from $2,000 to $1.3 million. The growth of most of these museums is a modern phenomenon.

For me, becoming a museum staff worker was not a typical career path. In the small town of my childhood, young African American boys could look forward to a lifetime of tending the hot blast furnaces in the local steel mill. African American girls, on the other hand, could anticipate experiencing a rite of passage at the age of thirteen, when they became "mother's helpers"—interim apprentices who prepared for work as full-time domestics in the homes of Bethlehem, Pennsylvania. I served my apprenticeship, and during that time,

I more than once pondered Countee Cullen's poem, "For a Lady I Know." In this poem a woman assumes that even in Heaven others of "her class" sleep late while youthful black angels must rise early to perform "celestial chores."[1]

A friend with whom I grew up and who is now a cardiac pediatrician in California characterizes as "expatriates" those African Americans of my generation who escaped into voluntary exile rather than live under an oppressive system. If that is true, then as an escapee, I somehow managed to travel to Washington, D.C., and to be in the right place at the right time when the Smithsonian Institution was about to initiate the Anacostia Museum, a neighborhood museum, in 1968.

At the Anacostia Museum, it was some time before anybody knew what to call me. When they looked at my job description and tried to decide what kind of performance guidelines to establish, they said that "the neighborhood concept of a museum is relatively novel. . . . Guidelines are generally lacking, requiring the incumbent to develop the education program without reference to comprehensive precedents." On the other hand, the Anacostia Museum's director, the late John Kinard, had rather clear guidelines. He recommended that the job candidate have mechanical or artistic ability so that he or she could build things and later explain how they worked to visitors. The leeway to build from the ground up allowed the museum to write its own scripts and the community to become a star in its own drama.

From the very beginning, the Anacostia Museum, inundated by children, exerted a nurturing influence in the community. I went to work every Saturday morning to get the children on the buses that took them to the Mall museums for classes. When I had weekend duty, as did each adult staff member, these children helped me wash the museum's front glass doors, sweep the outside pavement, vacuum the rug, and feed the animals in the zoo. We then waited impatiently for the museum's first visitors of the day, so that the children could guide them through "their" museum. The teenagers in the neighborhood literally helped to run the museum. I was the "other mother" to this extraordinary group of individuals who regularly helped to fabricate and to install exhibitions, to organize their own displays, to plan and to execute public programs, and even to raise enough money, with the neighborhood's help, to go abroad on two different occasions.

In addition to the female nurturers of these children, there were also strong, caring males on our staff who spent many hours guiding and counseling the children, as well as simply being there for them when they were needed. The women on staff were collaborators, not competitors, with their male colleagues. That was the only way the staff could transform an experimental project into a viable museum. The measure of our success has been shown to us repeatedly, as the following anecdotes suggest. Before the museum had a full-time janitorial service, a teenager working for us after school once refused to vacuum. The director insisted that he do so, and the boy ran home and returned with his mother, who demanded to know why her son had been asked to perform menial work. She and John Kinard had a long conversation, but she left unconvinced that her son was being trained to become a museum professional. Her son, however, remained to perform the task. Some years later, the boy returned. He had recently come back from Africa and was preparing for his second trip. He rolled with laughter when he recalled the story about the vacuum cleaner, and described how his year at the museum had changed not only his views about himself but also the course of his life.

Another example is a young woman who recently said, "The Anacostia Museum changed my life!" She had always disliked abstract art, but one day she came to the museum to see an exhibition of primarily abstract art. Next to the pieces on display were photographs of the African American artists who had created them and a statement that each artist had made about his or her work. She was astounded. For the first time in her life, the young woman began to examine closely every painting, because African Americans had not only created them but had said something understandable about each one.

She now regularly visits other art museums. Although she still does not like everything that she sees in all the museums, she says that she appreciates them much more than she had before.

The last example is my favorite. After a presentation to a group on our exhibition, "Blacks in the Westward Movement," I received a comment card that said, "You made me feel like a man." This was a rejoicing in pride and identity.

As I look at many of the younger African American women in the museum profession today, I feel great pride. They have such credentials as doctorates, business degrees, and master's in arts management. They are far better prepared than many of their predecessors were when they entered the museum world. A woman who recently came to volunteer at the museum exemplifies the extreme contrasts in the academic preparation of black women in museums. This woman had retired from the National Museum of Natural History, and just wanted something to occupy her time. We were told that she had begun work in the museum as an elevator operator more than forty years ago, when Washington, D.C., was a segregated city. After many years as an elevator operator, she secured a position as a cleaning woman in one of the labs. After working there for a while, she asked her supervisor what she could do to obtain a better job. He suggested that she return to school. She did, and because much of the literature she studied was in German, she began studying that language. Eventually she was hired as a museum specialist and became extremely proficient at the job, which included translating literature from German to English. By the time she retired, she had become one of the museum's most valued employees, and some of her co-workers referred to her as her supervisor's right hand.

Many black women who are new to the profession work in mainstream museums. This is more difficult psychologically for some, because it is quite different from working in an ethnic museum, in which on is surrounded by artifacts that celebrate one's particular heritage or identity. Problems arise because the power hierarchies of many of these museums, after all these years, still remain predominantly white and male. Some of my "sisters" tell me that they must spend half of their time justifying their programs and the other half insisting that their museums develop honest, balanced presentations. They ask, "How can we convince them that telling the African American story year-round—not just in February—is not only the appropriate thing to do but also the right thing to do?"

Both African American women and men tend to Africanize, or to reconstruct through an African worldview, Western cultural forms. From standard English, they created the black vernacular language. From Western music, they derived spirituals, jazz, blues, bebop, and rap. African American women will enter museums and apply the same powerful creativity exemplified in the evolution of African American culture. They will stretch our imaginations and cause us to examine our agendas. They will make museums user friendly, thereby humanizing them.

NOTE

1. Countee Cullen, "For a Lady I Know," in *My Soul's High Song: The Collected Works of Countee Cullen, Voice of the Harlem Renaissance,* ed. Gerald Early (New York: Anchor Books, 1991), 111.

PART 5

The Impact of Gender Perspectives

Museums as Educational Institutions

ALTHOUGH MUSEUMS have traditionally stated education as their primary mission, education has only recently become a major force in determining museum policies and programs. An American Association of Museums task force on education, as well as numerous symposia and educational roundtables, all indicate that education has become a key issue in museums (happily for those of us who fervently believe in the educational mission of museums). Education is coming to the forefront in overall museum planning and audience surveys, and educators have become part of the planning teams for exhibitions, publications, and many other programs.

In museum education, women's role is enlarging to include policy-making, both as trustees and as key administrative staff. Women have become even more prominent in the museum field as they have assumed new roles in addition to the traditional ones that they have always filled as lower-level museum education staff and museum volunteers.

The largest percentage of museum attendees have historically been women—especially before so many of them joined the work force—because museum hours were 10:00 A.M. to 5:00 P.M., were convenient for them and their children. Museum hours in the past favored the people who worked in museums. Our focus now, however, is more toward our audiences, and we realize the effect museum hours have on attendance patterns. Now that women participate nearly as much as men in the work force, it is obvious that we need to reexamine visitors' hours, in order to serve the public at their convenience.

Women have made substantial contributions in museum education. Since World War II the education department has become a primary location for women in museums—both in volunteer and professional capacities. The incentive that led women to take an active interest in museum education was both professional and personal, arising from a commitment to service and rewarding in the intellectual stimulation that it provided. Now women leaders in the museum education field are increasingly playing broader roles in policy-making and administration within many prominent institutions. In the art museums, for example, women educators such as Bonnie Pitman, Patterson Williams, Linda Downs, Meribell Parsons, Danielle Rice, and Cheryl McClenney Brooker are making important contributions. More and more women are also successful now as artists, having outlets for their work in business arrangements with important commercial galleries. They are playing major roles as gallery owners as well.

What has facilitated the emergence of a broader role for women museum educators? With education gaining due recognition, women are in a unique position to forecast and to lead museums in new directions. In the curatorial area, women's scholarship, background in education, and communication skills make them more than qualified to assume a prominent role. Other essays in this volume suggest that women as communicators are sensitive to people and potentially more articulate than men. Museums today, especially art museums, require that trustees and staff use their interpersonal skills in order to succeed and to thrive in an increasingly competitive and diverse environment. We tend to see museums not only as educational institutions and keepers of the flames but also in some ways as businesses. It is necessary then to be cognizant of every resource at our disposal, so that we may have greater impact in communicating our goals within that competitive setting. Within that context it is important that we not only recognize but also heed the individual and collective voices of women as museum professionals. It is fitting, therefore, to examine the important roles women play and have played in museum education. It is important that the voices of women be heard, because of the strength that they provide with their individual professional contributions.

Roger Mandle

A Recent History of Women Educators in Art Museums

Linda Downs

THIS ESSAY aims to survey the recent history of women educators in art museums. Women in academia have been fairly well studied, but the book on women as educators in art museums is yet to be written. Three main sources exist. Terry Zeller's essay in *Museum Education: History, Theory, and Practice* provides some rudimentary information on important contributions by women in art museum education.[1] Two other books are older and helpful but focus on academia: *Women as Interpreters of the Visual Arts, 1820–1979* and *Women in Academia: Progress and Prospectus.*[2] I combine the information from these books with my own research to present a perspective on the development of women in the field of art history and art museum education.

From the 1820s to the 1890s the concept of women as guardians of culture was predominant in the United States. Women were designated to contribute to the community's cultural life. Although they had no professional status in either museums or academia, they did contribute vastly to scholarship in art history by translating scholarly texts and producing popular histories, guidebooks, and monographs on individual artists, as well as working on collections or documents and studies in iconography, architectural history, and criticism.

At the turn of the century women began entering the art museum profession at junior levels, emphasizing primarily research rather than acquisitions and donor development. In academia women's colleges were leaders in providing visual arts courses for women. These courses, however, were rarely offered in major universities. Many art museum professionals are aware of the museum studies course initiated by Paul Sachs at Harvard University in 1921, but little is known of the two courses set up as early as 1910 by women that had preceded Sachs's course by several years. Wellesley College offered a course taught by Myrtella Avery, and the Pennsylvania Museum (which later became the Philadelphia Museum of Art) offered one by Sarah York Stevenson. Such museum studies courses produced women who were professionally trained at an early stage in the history of American art museums.

From the 1890s to the 1930s women entered the art museum profession on unequal terms with their male colleagues. They took inferior positions and were paid less. Their contributions continued to be in art historical and critical texts, the results of solitary endeavors. There was no institutional structure that would help women progress in the museum environment. From 1905 to 1945 only ten women attained full curatorial status at major U.S. art museums, and nearly all of them were single or married without children.

The discrimination women encountered within art museums did not prevent some from making important contributions to the development of museum education. Florence N. Levy, of the Metropolitan Museum of Art, wrote extensively on museum education. She surveyed museum education programs, categorizing them as being for the public's enjoyment, for the advancement of artists and art students, for informing experts, for serving industry, and for introducing children to art history. (Besides serving industry, women today are still working in the similar areas.) Molly Godwin, who worked at the Toledo Museum of Art, wrote *The Museum Educates,* one of the most complete statements on museum education philosophy and practice in the thirties.[3] In the forties one of the most outstanding art museum educators was Katherine Kuh, at the Chicago Art Institute. She set up an experimental gallery that promoted visual literacy rather than verbal-based learning in art museums. Through her exhibitions, publications, and lectures, she made substantial contributions to the art museum educational field.

In the sixties and seventies the women's movement focused on gender inequities, support networks, and neglected art historical topics such as feminist scholarship, the imagery of women, and erotic art. The revolution that occurred in academia, however, did not occur in art museums, where only quiet changes took place. A conference on women in the arts was held at the Corcoran Gallery of Art in 1972. At that conference I first became aware of the artists and feminist activists Miriam Schapiro and Judy Chicago. I also remember being shocked to see women in black leather jackets, chains, and shaved heads at the conference, but I was invigorated by the conference's feminist agenda and its expression of frustration and anger with the art profession, as well as the search for new directions. In the same year the Women's Caucus for the Arts, which has had an enormous influence on feminist art history and issues related to women in the arts, was founded. In 1973 the Education Committee of the American Association of Museums was formed by Bonnie Pitman, Elaine Gurian, Adrienne Horn, and other women. This committee has since contributed to the professionalism of museum education.

While the changes that occurred for women in academia in the seventies were more dramatic than those in art museums, the number of women in professional positions in both settings remained comparable. In 1978 a survey of major universities indicated that 56 percent of the doctorates in art history were awarded to women, but only 17 percent of them became tenured faculty. (The statistics have changed little since then). In 1970 few women had attained senior positions in major art museums, and as of 1978 only one woman, Jean Sutherland Boggs, was the director of a major American art museum. In the eighties, however, that number radically changed. According to the Committee of Women Art Museum Directors, in 1990 one hundred and fifty women were directors of art museums throughout the country, out of one thousand art museums nationwide.

Much information has still to be gathered to provide a complete portrait of the current status of women in art museums. The American Association of Museums, the College Art Association, the Women's Caucus for the Arts, and several other organizations do not gather statistics on women in art museums. The only statistical source I have found are the reports from the Office of Equal Opportunity at the Smithsonian Institution. Even though these statistics represent a small sample, the data may suggest women's status in museums nationwide. At the Smithsonian Institution, out of 3,391 total professional, technical, and administrative positions, 35 percent, are filled by females. Of its 471 professional positions, 152 or 33 percent are held by women. In comparison, the number of women holding full-time positions in academia has increased by 27 percent in the last decade; however, tenured positions have not increased, and the salary differential between men and women has actually risen by 20 percent in the last decade.

Female trustees potentially have an enormous voice and influence in art museums. A 1985 study of trustees in academic institutions shows that female trustees demonstrate great concern for social issues and women's issues in terms of leadership, role models, and part-time matriculation, but they are not in positions of power on the boards. Studies of trustees in academia have indicated a conflictual situation for women, who come to the boards well-educated and insightful but generally not holding the positions that they could. They do not, for example, chair boards or head finance committees. Trustee boards that have the most diverse age, gender, racial makeup, and political viewpoints were the ones most successful in surviving major institutional crises. Diversity brings strength, and fresh energy brings new insights.

Women have made significant contributions to art historical scholarship, art museum curatorship, and education in art museums during the short time that they have held professional status in academia and art museums. To look at the most extreme case, the first American museum was founded in 1779 in Charleston, South Carolina. The history of U.S. museums is thus 214 years old. Women's professional status in art museums began after World War II—encompassing only a forty-five-year history. Some historians believe that most female art historians, curators, and educators have adopted the methodology of mainstream art history and administration by not having "feminine characteristics" in their work. Others believe that women have addressed the popularization and socialization of art more than the aesthetics of art. We need a broader historical perspective before such generalizations can legitimately be made, and we need to collect statistics to assess the current situation. The next survey of the American Association of Museums should include statistics on women in the profession.

There are various academic programs for women who are interested in becoming administrators. I know of no such course in the museum world, in which it is needed. Women also have an obligation to assume leadership positions and to take affirmative action seriously in programming and in hiring. Women's studies should also be incorporated into museum studies courses. The Association of American Colleges' Project on the Status and Education of Women, which was a consciousness-raising effort to reduce the problem of subtle discrimination, provides an excellent model. There is an enormous amount of work to be done in piecing our history together and in assuming leadership roles in the profession.

NOTES

1. Terry Zeller, "The Historical and Philosophical Foundations of Art Museum Education in America," in *Museum Education, History, Theory, and Practice,* ed. Nancy Berry and Susan Mayer (Reston, Va.: National Art Education Association, 1989).

2. See Claire Richter Sherman and Adele M. Holcomb, eds., *Women as Interpreters of the Visual Arts, 1820–1979* (Westport, Conn: Greenwood Press, 1981); and Marian K. Chamberlain, ed., *Women in Academia: Progress and Prospectus* (New York: Russell Sage Foundation, 1988).

3. See Molly Ohl Godwin, *The Museum Educates* (Toledo, Ohio: Toledo Museum of Art, 1936).

Interpreting Gender Perspectives

Malcolm Arth

I AM uncomfortable with our tendency to stereotype groups. Since there is diversity in every group, neither women nor men are a monolithic group. Phyllis Schlafly is not Gloria Steinem, and I am not Ronald Reagan. We have to be cautious when we make generalizations. It is something we all need to remind ourselves about periodically.

I announced in 1988 that I will retire at age sixty-one, so in 1990 I will have a year to go. At this time, late in one's professional life, one is allowed to look around and to reflect. So I have chosen to be informal and reflective in my remarks.

One of things that I address is the role of the museum educator as a scholar. In museums the major mechanism for communicating with the public is through the exhibition format. The question that must be raised is: How effectively can the world of ideas be communicated through exhibitions? I have always had serious reservations about our ability to communicate information through the techniques that we have developed, hoping that the means to convey abstract ideas and intellectual issues using methods other than the label and the object would be developed.

Museum education departments are places in which women have had power and a special role. Education departments, which are often relegated to the basements of our institutions, have been and frequently still are staffed with volunteers, a largely female group that is often unpaid. It is important not to stereotype education departments as all being staffed primarily by unpaid women volunteers. It is important, however, to acknowledge that women have played an important role in those divisions, and it is not an accident that education departments are low in the hierarchy of priorities within our institutions.

Marcia Tucker's essay, "From Theory to Practice: Correcting Inequalities," contends that our labels [text to exhibitions] should not be written in stone, because they could present alternative explanations, majority and minority views, or conflicting interpretations by fellow curators or by colleagues in other institutions. The notion that there are several perspectives or alternative views is intrinsic to an intellectual approach. Libraries, universities, or any place in which scholarship occurs would be unimaginable without that principal. Only in museums do we find an arrogance that permits the one-sided view that an audience interprets as "the truth" rather than as one person's view, one institution's view, one sexist view, or one racist view.

Kendall Taylor's essay, "Pioneering Efforts of Early Museum Women," gives an excellent historical overview of women in museums; however, I take exception to her categorization of women. Taylor remarks that many of the great women curators and directors of the early part of this century were unmarried and that their job was their life. Similarly, Jean Weber in her essay, "Changing Roles and Attitudes," observes that these women were probably "a little bit lonely." Such interpretations demean these women as individuals. We do not know whether they had substantial social lives outside their museum work, but I assume that they did. One woman frequently mentioned is Margaret Mead, who had three husbands and, as we learned from her daughter's book, also had a number of female lovers, the first being fellow anthropologist Ruth Fulton Benedict. Benedict and Mead are examples of people, whose lives we know posthumously, who were high achievers and extraordinary contributors to our profession but also had private lives. Such women should not be stereotyped as "those wonderful unmarried ladies." Whether they went home to man, woman, or beast—or just went home—it is a disservice to view them as being solely dedicated to their profession and having no other lives. Some of them may have been lonely, and some may have indeed had their job dominate their lives.

Another issue to examine is museums as conservative institutions. Museums are not at the forefront of social change—neither civil rights nor women's issues. If we look worldwide, we see institutions that play a strong role in social change. Whether discussing the political upheavals at Tiananmen Square or in the Czech Republic, Hungary, or Russia, museums will not be mentioned, because they are not involved as leaders. In our country museums are rarely on the cutting edge, but universities, students, churches, military institutions, and political organizations are. Museums have thus played only a minor role as agents of change. Twenty years ago, when I left academia and entered the museum world, I wrote an article in which I described museums as "timid" in comparison with universities. I continue to see that same timidity—that willingness to react but not to initiate action and that trembling at the thought of someone raising a question that might embarrass somebody else. We must overcome that and play stronger roles.

We are currently living in a period of political and social conservatism. It will not last, neither will the period of liberal politics and social approaches that will surely follow it. We must, however, recognize the period in which we now live and accept the responsibilities that it imposes upon us. There is increasing racial polarization in our major cities. The feminist label that was so proudly worn by men and women is less eagerly acclaimed by both men and women today. The hard-won rights to abortion are being challenged. There is great stress and conflict, no matter on what side of those issues you stand. Museums can play a role.

One of the important issues raised is that of a feminist perspective in all our work—in exhibition development and interpretation, in educational programs, and even in the nature of the research we do. We are doing better now than we were. Salaries have improved. Even though there are few people of color and about forty women among the 170 members of the Association of Art Museum Directors, that compares favorably with the situation ten or twenty years ago.

We have to be careful to separate our statistics from the feminist perspective that has been clearly delineated; that perspective is extremely important and potentially capable of contributing to our profession. We should not, however, begin thinking exclusively one way or the other. We need to come together.

Evaluating the Ethics and Consciences of Museums

Robert Sullivan

IN THIS essay, I make two arguments. First, I argue that museums are moral educators and must speak with confidence and competence on such ethical issues as gender and race equity.[1] As educational institutions, we are necessarily agents of change, not only changing the knowledge, beliefs, attitudes, and feelings of our individual visitors but also affecting the moral ecology of the communities that we serve. The pattern of our decision making in our governance policies, hiring practices, and collection and interpretation programs sends value-laden messages to our communities about what we consider to be worthwhile and just.

Second, based on the extent to which one race and/or gender dominates museums' governance, policies, practices, and programs, I argue that museums are generally racist and sexist institutions. I do not contend that as institutions museums overall are maliciously racist and sexist, although I believe that there have been incidents of overt racism or sexism. I believe, however, that we are thoughtlessly racist and sexist institutions. It is not that we do not care but that we lack systematic ways to assess and to evaluate our flaws in order to direct cumulative change in our activities.

Museums tend to be what I call "episodic institutions," having episodes of success but having difficulty sustaining longitudinal change. With this in mind, rather than merely describing the problem, I propose criteria for systematically assessing sex equity issues in permanent exhibits. I hope that these criteria may assist us in developing professional standards that might lead to longitudinal change in our institutions and ultimately in societal behaviors.[2]

THE MUSEUM AS MORAL EDUCATOR

Museums are ritual places in which societies make visible what they value. Through the selection and preservation of artifacts, specimens, and documents, museums begin to define for their societies what is consequential, valuable, and suitable as evidence of the past. Through their presentation and interpretation of this evidence, museums define not only what is memorable but also how it is to be remembered. Museums are thus unavoidably linked with their cultural settings. They are a collective self-reflection culminating in the maintenance, sustenance, and presentation of a cultural identity, as well as the embodiment of cultural values and attitudes believed to be important. Museums thus reveal their own moral nature, competence, and maturity in their decisions about what and how to transmit social values and ideas. While museums often claim to be value-neutral, nonmoral, and nonpolitical in intent, in their actual practice and behavior, they are moralizing institutions, reflecting as well as shaping their communities' moral ecology.

The core of museums' moral dimension is located in the decisions and the choices that they must make and then visibly enact: What do they choose to collect and not to collect? What themes and materials are exhibited and under what interpretive conditions? What audience or audiences are courted and welcomed in the museum, and what audience or audiences are ignored? Who is given comfortable psychological, intellectual, and physical access to the museum and its resources? What programmatic themes are addressed? How is the museum governed? Who is on the board? Who is on the staff? These choices are value laden and, combined, establish a pattern of policies, procedures, and public programs that define and communicate the museum's norms, ethics, and moral identity—its compelling sense of self. This contention that museums, because of their educational and social intent and institutional choices, cannot be value-neutral or nonmoral in their actions and behaviors, suggests that the question to be addressed is not *should* museums be moral educators but *how* museums should be involved in moral education. How can museums develop a conscious moral purpose based on appropriate aims, concepts, and content? If the goal of museums as educators is to assist in developing the whole person—his or her knowledge, attitudes, beliefs, and feelings—then how should a museum develop the intellectual, aesthetic, and moral judgments of its visitors and communities? What *ought* a museum do?

SEX EQUITY AND THE PERMANENT EXHIBIT

Permanent exhibitions at the New York State Museum are those that are expected to remain in place, relatively unchanged, for forty years. It is not accidental that such exhibits last for about one generation, before their style and content are declared old-fashioned, irrelevant, or even unethical. As assumptions and attitudes toward what is valuable in history or the natural environment change, exhibits are no longer in touch with their community's expectations.

In 1976 the New York State Museum began its ongoing efforts of planning, designing, and installing 120,000 square feet of new permanent exhibitions in its new home in the Cultural Education Center. Determining the overarching theme that would drive the exhibitions' aims and content was critical, since this point of view would define what themes would be excluded in the exhibits as well as those that would be included. The museum decided to abandon the traditional, discipline-based approach that treats human history and natural history as separate subjects. A more integrated, holistic style was chosen to address the central questions: How do human activity and the natural environment interact, and what are the consequences of one on the other?

Of particular concern was the issue of fair representation of race and gender in New York State's development. To address this issue, a sex equity committee was formed to examine exhibit themes, linguistics, and design. This committee was voluntary and composed of equal numbers of men and women. Formation of this internal advisory group resulted from a growing awareness of patterns of bias that had minimized the visibility of women and minorities in educational materials, including museum exhibits. Its draft report identified six forms of gender bias:

Invisibility

Certain groups are underrepresented in exhibits and other instructional materials. The omission of women and minority groups is very damaging because it implies that these groups are of less value and significance in our society.

Stereotyping

By assigning traditional and rigid roles or attributes to a group, exhibits and instructional materials stereotype and limit the abilities and potential of that group. Stereotyping denies students a knowledge of the diversity, complexity, and variation of any group of individuals. Children who see themselves portrayed only in stereotypical ways may internalize these stereotypes and fail to develop their own unique abilities, interests, and full potential.

Imbalance/Selectivity

Exhibits and instructional materials perpetuate bias by presenting only one interpretation of an issue, situation, or a group of people. This imbalanced account restricts students' knowledge about the varied perspectives that might apply to a particular situation. Through selective presentation, instructional materials frequently present an unrealistic portrayal of our history and our contemporary life experience. Controversial topics are glossed over, and discussions of discrimination and prejudice are avoided. This unrealistic coverage denies children the information they need to recognize, to understand, and perhaps some day to conquer the problems that plague our society.

Fragmentation/Isolation

By separating issues related to minorities and women from the main body of the text, exhibits and instructional materials imply that these issues are less important and not a part of the cultural mainstream.

Linguistic Bias

Curricular materials reflect the discriminatory nature of our language. Masculine terms and pronouns, ranging from "our forefathers" to the generic "he," subtly ignore references to the participation of women in our society. Further, occupations such as "mailman" are given masculine labels that deny the legitimacy of women working in these fields. Imbalance of word order and lack of parallel terms that refer to females and males are also forms of linguistic bias.

The internal advisory group recommended the following criteria for evaluating museum exhibits, programs, and publications for gender equity:

Robert Sullivan

Invisibility

1. Are equally meaningful roles given to both men and women? What effort has been made to represent men and women as having equal status: professional, social, economic, etc.?
2. Do the visible credits on the exhibit, film, or program reflect the broad range of individuals who contributed to the product?
3. Are men and women both equally represented by the artifacts? By people? By voice?
4. Are quotes and anecdotes from women in history and from important living women used as frequently as those from men?
5. If men and women have different roles, are these separate roles shown as being equally important to the overall development of culture?
6. Have opportunities been missed to present sex-fair images?

Stereotyping

1. When people are presented visually in roles, is an effort made to avoid stereotyping their behaviors and aspirations? For example, are women always presented as nurturers and men as builders or persons involved in technology?
2. Are opportunities taken to give examples of both men and women in significant roles that do not contradict historical fact?
3. Unless there is a specific reason for not doing so (i.e., historical example), are both sexes portrayed from similar attitudinal perspectives (e.g., humor, satire, respect, etc.)?
4. Is an effort made to avoid using only pastel colors and fuzzy line definition to illustrate females and only strong colors and bold lines to portray males?
5. Do graphs and charts use other than stereotypical stick figures?
6. Do the materials indicate mutual respect among the characters through their posture, clothing, and gestures?
7. Are physical and emotional stereotypes avoided? Is an effort made to avoid showing men only as vigorous and powerful and women only as delicate and fragile?
8. Do illustrations include other than young, attractive, and preferred body types?

Imbalance/Selectivity

1. Do artifacts reflect varieties of populations and subcultures whenever possible?
2. If artifactual evidence is not available, how are unrepresented populations accounted for?
3. How is the planning staff of the exhibit, program, or film balanced for gender and other constituent group representation to provide a variety of experiences and perspectives?
4. Are experts such as sociologists brought in at appropriate times so that the full spectrum of peoples contributing to our society's evolution is reflected in all aspects on the museum?
5. Does the material presented reflect other value systems besides that of the majority white male culture?
6. If historical bias exists, how does the exhibit, film, or program, acknowledge this limitation? (E.g., in the past women couldn't attach their names to literature, music, inventions, etc.)

Unreality

1. What effort is made to discuss, to exhibit, and/or to encourage programs on controversial topics such as discrimination and prejudice?
2. When a historically biased situation is cited or represented, how is it qualified as past values that are no longer acceptable?

Fragmentation

1. Have certain issues that are gender-related been separated from the main body of materials, implying that these issues are less important?

Linguistic Bias

1. Is the generic "she" used where the antecedent is stereotypically female (e.g., "the housekeeper . . . she")?
2. Is the generic "he" used to include both males and females when gender is unspecified?

3. Does the material use sex-fair language initially and then slip into the use of the generic "he" (e.g., "A worker can have union dues deducted from his pay.")?

4. Are women identified by their own names rather than their husband's names (e.g., Madame Pierre Curie, Mrs. F. D. Roosevelt)?

5. Are nonparallel terms used in referring to males and females (e.g., Dr. Jones and his secretary, Ellen; Senator Kennedy and Mrs. Ghandi)?

6. When referring to both sexes, does the male term consistently precede the female (e.g., he and she, boys and girls)?

7. Are occupational titles used with -man as the suffix (e.g., chairman, businessman)?

8. When an individual holds a nontraditional job, is there unnecessary focus on the person's sex (e.g., the woman doctor, the male nurse)?

9. Are women described in terms of their appearance or marital and familial status, while men are described in terms of accomplishments or titles (e.g., Senator Kennedy and Golda Meir, mother of two)?

10. Is the text consistent with the illustrations in terms of sex fairness?

The New York State Museum is now in the process of applying these criteria to its existing exhibits and programs, as well as to those in progress. Already, the linguistics of the museum has changed. The portrayal of the division of labor and women's role in prehistoric Native American cultures has been refined for our upcoming life groups. The posture, gestures, and attitudes of figures in these life groups have been more consciously considered. A heightened awareness exists among staff of the unconscious, or at least preconscious, prejudices and stereotyping that can be packaged into every aspect of exhibit scripting and design.

Identifying what is intolerable to us and combating it is a hopeful beginning. We agree that sexism, racism, and inequity are intolerable to us, but the other half of this concluding strategy is "acting against" them. According to Susan B. Anthony,

> Cautious, careful, people, always casting about to preserve their reputation and social standing never can bring about a reform. Those who must be really in earnest must be willing to be anything or nothing in the world's estimation, and publicly and privately, in season and out, avow their sympathy with despised and persecuted ideas and their advocates, and bear the consequences.[3]

In the belief that Anthony is fundamentally correct, that reform of institutions comes from committed, passionate, risk-taking behavior by individual staff members. I suggest a list of individual acts that we can follow in order to initiate change:

1. Write a critique of one exhibition and submit it to your supervisor.
2. Refuse to distribute—especially to teachers and children—learning materials, brochures, and any literature that uses sexist or racist language.
3. Form a voluntary equity committee.
4. Fight for pay equity for undervalued staff and categories of staff (such as clerical staff and instructors); and refuse raises until pay equity is reached.
5. Write and submit a report and recommendations on specific equity issues in your institution.
6. Confront positively all sexist and racist remarks.
7. Remove office materials that are sexist or racist.
8. Announce that you are a feminist (especially if you are a man).

NOTES

1. I join these two issues only because they are generally interrelated in this society and are essentially moral issues with related principles and concepts of equity, justice, and empathy.

2. As an aside, I think it is self-evident that complete societal change, which is preceded by institutional change, is precipitated by the insistent moral commitment of key individuals within those institutions. We now clearly understand the need to address racism and sexism in our economic, judicial, and educational institutions, but relatively little attention has been paid to our cultural institutions. Sadly, this is probably because neither museum professionals nor the society in general take museums seriously as agents of change. Museums have enormous potential as "thermostatic" institutions that counteract dangerously prevalent and dominating ways the society transmits and receives information and experience—but this is the topic for another essay.

3. Ida Husted Harper, *The Life and Work of Susan B. Anthony, Including Public Addresses, Her Own Letters . . . during Fifty Years* (Indianapolis: Hollenbeck Press, 1898), 1:197.

An Inside View

Margery Gordon

WHAT ROLE are museums playing today? In their essays, Malcolm Arth and Robert Sullivan question whether the role of museums needs to change. They ask whether museums can be perceived as timid institutions or energetic, driving forces that help shape our world. Sullivan especially notes that museums should be important educational institutions, relying on new exhibits to present ideas and scholarship that are on the cutting edge.

Although I have worked in the art, anthropology, and environmental science fields, designing educational programs for more than sixty museum exhibits, only a few of the exhibits produced have taken a strong stance on or even attempted to examine currently controversial issues. I would have hoped for more experimentation and leadership.

As a woman who has been in the museum profession for many years, I suspect that there is probably some bias here, since the largest percentage of professional staff in museums in public programming and education tends to be female. Men who are museum educators often are in top positions and generally make the crucial decisions.

In the introduction to this book, Mary Schmidt Campbell discusses an important theme—that of personal achievement in contrast with working within a group to find solutions together. Sullivan also refers to the collective voice that goes beyond creating programs to encompass the self-awareness of the institution. I believe that the personal side of oneself, which Campbell sees as detrimental to group dynamics, can merge with the group-oriented aspect of oneself, providing a meaningful voice that does not sacrifice personal goals. For women—especially for those in museum education departments—this is a real dilemma, because they are often unheard. The collective voice speaks out, but does not carry any weight for women, whether they serve on the board, participate in organizational decisions, or work on an education staff.

Several years ago, members of the education staff were involved in an exhibition on archeological finds in Caesarea, Israel, that had extensive label copy and photographs that were crucial to the concepts stressed in the show. When the final plans were made, it was apparent to the educators, all of whom were women, that the signs should be moved from the entrance, so that visitors would have more space to read and then to walk through the exhibition. The designers and curators, all of whom were men, failed to see the wisdom in this decision, although the educators had worked with this same space many times before. They declined to implement the change. On the night of the opening, four hundred people were backed up at the entrance to the exhibit, because they wanted to read the copy. On the morning after the opening, the signs were moved. The designers and curators could have avoided this occurrence, if they had listened to the collective voice of the female educators.

The education staff at the National Museum of Natural History is often on the planning committees for exhibits, public programs, and other issues of importance. Because this is a science institution in which there are more male than female curators and technicians, the women, especially in the education department, are not the ones who can easily effect change. Women educators are often included at the end rather than at the beginning of the decision-making process. Their involvement in the planning of an exhibit—seeing that it works for the public; responding to cultural, gender, and racial issues; and making the research intelligible and relevant to diverse people—requires that they be involved with the decision-making process from the start, if women are to emerge with a more powerful voice collectively.

As women, we need to draw fundraisers into the educational process. We need to be involved in long-range planning in which we can voice our needs for public programs, educational training, effective exhibit design, and publications that are adjuncts to the catalog. We need to feel as if we are part of the process and to become integral to the governance of the institution. A big question arises here: How can a woman with unique experiences and expertise feel integral to the process, participate in group decisions, and still realize individual goals? It is not an easy question to answer. While still encouraging the collective mentality, we all need to recognize and to respect individual talents and to not be afraid of allowing strong, independent, and creative women to have outlets.

In her essay, "Pioneering Efforts of Early Museum Women," Kendall Taylor names outstanding women in the museum field who were respected and known for their individual expertise and their forceful personalities. As Taylor's essay indicates, women who rose in the museum profession were often those who stood out from the group and realized their personal goals. I do not know the best way for one to achieve personal goals when working in a group, but I do know that it is important for groups to accommodate people who are not team players, as they aspire for individual goals. For women, this is especially true, since they are often grouped together and expected to behave politely. It is also as a group, however, that women can sometimes have a voice and empower themselves in order to become more instrumental in institutional changes.

Institutions should listen to women because women have a long history as nurturers and caretakers. As such, women can affect the decision-making process and the design programs and spaces that make a museum special to a visitor. Perhaps it is the experience of being a homemaker or caretaker that reminds women museum professionals not only to impart information but also to do so in a hospitable manner. This may entail the museum staff serving cookies and tea to teachers during Saturday morning workshops. This may also entail providing enough seats for families or group visitors, so that everyone can sit as they relax and regroup. We can effectively use our experience as women so that the museum is perceived as a vital place in the community.

If we are going to make museum programs within the museum effective and useful to people of other cultures, we must listen to their needs and their collective voice and include them in our processes. If we are going to serve urban African Americans or Hispanics, we must first know what their interests are and what we can do together. We must also be willing to make them feel comfortable in the museum, so that they can respond positively.

I am on a Smithsonian Institution committee that focuses on programs for Hispanic Heritage Month. We have been discussing whether we should do programs bilingually or in either Spanish or English. If there is little money available, we have to decide what our priorities are. If we cannot pay for Spanish interpreters, we must find alternatives with the community's help. Because so many of the local Hispanics are working-class people who do not have time to volunteer, we must offer some of the programs in the evenings or on the weekends. We must also rely on assistance from the embassies and other groups in the private sector. We may even create a new team to find solutions as a collective voice.

The National Museum of Natural History should emphasize diversity in its hiring practices, employing not only people from diverse cultural and ethnic groups but also and especially women whenever possible. I hope, however, that this is not the only way the museum will reach out. There are many people on the staff who, if given the opportunity, have the knowledge and the experience to make critical and effective decisions.

The Smithsonian Institution has been successful in fostering cultural equity. Several committees have been designed to address the needs of African Americans, Hispanics, Native Americans, and Asian Pacific peoples. These committees have been able to effectively increase the awareness of diverse cultural heritages. Here the collective voice has been very positive. Each committee found ways to work together as a collective voice in order to publicize their events. Programs were marketed under the Institution's new image as a university on the Mall. Museum programs are often now referred to as pan-Institutional events held on "the campus."

Some inroads have been made with celebrations of Women's History Month. Gender perspectives on issues and exhibits, however, should be represented throughout the year rather than limited to one month. Celebration of women's history is not the answer to gender equity but a means through which the collective female voice can speak out and plan successful programs.

Do outreach activities address the uninitiated museum visitors, or do they focus on programs for those who are already habitual museum visitors? Exhibits and programs with specialized themes are often perceived as only being for a specific audience. Performances from other cultures, especially those that are not in English, also tend to limit the audience. It should not be that only African Americans attend a museum exhibit on black churches. Because museums have long excluded these minorities, there is now a growing sense of pride when the involvement is more apparent and the focus more direct. How we advertise our programs to different ethnic or women's groups can make a difference. Seeking support in outreach endeavors from women's associations and university groups may be helpful.

I think that we often talk in psychological or abstract terms about what we would like to see rather than realistically assessing the situation. We must take a hard look at existing programs and not be afraid to rewrite or to eliminate labels or textual materials that are sexist or exclusionary. I am not suggesting that we give up or even compromise our values, but that we be realistic about what we can effectively achieve in the museums and work more toward those ends. We as women educators should feel proud that we have contributed to the system and have enacted major changes despite the odds. I also think we should feel proud as women, realize our potentialities, work to maintain open minds, and see gender perspectives as only one of the issues that we must address in the future.

PART 6

The Impact of the Future on Museums

Societal and Technological Changes

AS WE move through the nineties and plan for the next century, there are many significant societal changes that are occurring. Our population is becoming older, better educated, and much more culturally diverse. Our schools are due for a major overhaul. The technology and information explosion is overwhelming. Life on earth is endangered ecologically. How can museums help to provide appropriate and inspiring solutions to these problems? Will gender make a difference in our approach to these issues and affect their potential solutions? Can women assume leadership roles? These are some of the questions that the following essays address.

Janet W. Solinger

In Preparation for the Future

Heather Paul

AS THE United States nears the twenty-first century, there is a sense that we are in the midst of a profound restructuring of society, institutions, and lifestyles. Museums, long regarded as only preservers of the past, are now also barometers of the future. How successfully museums adapt to the rapid changes inside and outside their walls will determine their futures. Like museums, women will face increasing threats, as well as opportunities to invent a preferred future—one that is quite different from the past and even the present.

Elizabeth Cady Stanton had no choice but to see the future as hopeful. In *History of Woman Suffrage*, she wrote:

> Thus far women have been mere echoes of men. Our laws and constitutions, our creeds and codes, and the customs of social life are all of masculine origin. The true woman is yet a dream of the future.[1]

Testimony from museum professionals confirms that strong patriarchal echoes are still resonating through museum life, and true equity for women is still more dream than reality.

It is interesting to note today's contrasting images of tomorrow's woman. In the novel *A Handmaid's Tale*, Margaret Atwood paints a bleak future of a world that has become polluted and corrupt, with only a few fertile women to play out lives as prized slaves.[2] In contrast with Atwood's representation, there are two best-sellers on the future that depict rosy scenarios. Marvin Cetron's *American Renaissance* and John Naisbitt's *Megatrends 2000* offer Pollyannish notions of women's marvelous rise in corporate boardrooms, the existence of wondrous birth-control technology, and other theories of technoandrogyny.[3]

No one can forecast women's futures. Instead there are alternative scenarios that offer as frightening or as fulfilling a future that we as a society choose to make. Women in museums similarly have choices ranging from remaining silently exploited in reactionary institutions to creating museum spaces of their own, as Marcia Tucker has done with the New Museum of Contemporary Art in New York City. In this essay, I examine the trends and the impact of these broad forces for change that are affecting women and museums.

DEMOGRAPHICS

The most obvious and predictable future trend is the nation's shifting demographic composition. The United States is aging and changing color. By 2000, the median age of Americans will have risen from thirty in 1980 to thirty-six and a half. The greatest population growth in the next decade will be among thirty-five-to fifty-four-year-olds. The second fastest-growing group is those over seventy-five years old, which will grow by 28 percent in this same period. As 77 million baby boomers move into their middle and later years, they will have as dramatic an effect on aging as they did on other phases of the life cycle. Museums of the twenty-first century, as well as many other institutions, will be much more conscious of these aging Americans' special needs. Museums will be increasingly accommodating to the needs of this aging population— for example, providing facilities to those of them with sight and hearing impairments. These efforts will coincide with the growing awareness of the rights of people with disabilities.

Along with anxious policy analysts in the Social Security Administration, others are fascinated by the prospect of reinventing aging—especially for women. Women are still outliving men by the average of five years and spending many more years alone. The specter of becoming one of the frail elderly is nothing any of us desire. Better health care and use of women's flexibility and adaptability to new circumstances, however, could result in a totally new way of growing old—especially for women.

One of the most wonderful aspects of an exhibition I saw at the Corcoran Gallery of Art, "I Dream a World," was its emphasis on older black women. In stark black and white photography, these women's gray hair, lined faces, and sinewy hands were blown up before me; and they were absolutely beautiful. In 1969 I experienced this same sense of the possibilities of aging. Sitting at Margaret Mead's feet at a post-lecture event in Cincinnati, I thought, "This is how I want to grow old." In Mead, good works and accomplishment had combined with age to create something much finer than sheer youth.

The boomers are entering their peak earning and spending years, and it will be incumbent on museums to gain this cohort's loyalties by justifying their existence before they can anticipate significant financial support. There will be many causes and institutions vying for this same support. Museums will have to prove their worthiness for their share of the baby boomers' philanthropy.

As the boomers age, all of America is becoming much more heterogeneous. Currently one in four Americans are racial or ethnic minorities; by 2000 the ratio will be one in three. These facts, compounded by a decreased population-growth rate of less than 1 percent a year, will mean that minorities and women will receive special attention, especially in the workplace and in museums. As Rowena Stewart suggests in "The Empowerment of African American Museums," people want to see reflections of themselves in museums. According to marketers, we live in an increasingly consumer-driven society. One-third of the nation's Hispanics, Asian Americans, or African Americans will simply not visit a museum that in no way mirrors their own experiences.

SEXUAL POLITICS OF THE WORKPLACE

The U.S. work force will be dramatically affected by the growing majority of women and minorities. Over 60 percent of all women will work outside their homes, and a little more than half the work force will be composed of women by the year 2000. Women's entrance into the work force is a long-lasting trend that is evident throughout the world. Their presence will permanently change the nature of work for both men and women. Issues of maternity or paternity leave, day-care subsidies, flextime, and shortened workweeks are not fads but permanent adjustments to the workplace. In the future these options will not be regarded as part of a "mommy track" that, when chosen by some women, discriminates against those women who are climbing the conventional career ladder. Instead, "parent-track" work patterns will become acceptable for those in their childbearing years.

The sexual politics of museums' organizational cultures are also changing, albeit slowly. The old hierarchies of museum life—such as male curators and directors maintained by countless female assistants, and the sexist exhibit practices of art galleries—may be slow to disappear, but their disappearance is finally inevitable. The essayists in this volume testify to women's new authority and power in museum life. In the short term, however, progress is not always apparent. It is important to develop incremental signposts to measure our advancement. For example, the next steps should be consciously different and better—perhaps more action strategies, more male involvement, and more task forces committed to activism.

Women's gradual progress toward economic independence is also rearranging opportunities and constraints in gender relations. Heterosexual relationships are growing increasingly unstable. Divorce rates, which still reflect and predict the dissolution of one out of two marriages, show no indication of changing in the next few decades. The forecasts suggest that millions more Americans will spend more of their lives unmarried and raising children alone. Like other institutions, museum employment practices must accommodate the needs of single-parent female or male staff members. We know that major institutions such as libraries are starting to confront the reality of their role as after-school baby-sitters or midday havens for the aged. It is possible that museums of the future will also more deliberately support families with actual after-school programs or better hours in the early evenings for working parents or retired older persons.

VALUE TRANSFORMATIONS: THE COMING DECADE OF SOCIAL RESPONSIBILITY

The single most important trend between now and 2000 may be the shift in the national mood toward "the assumption of responsibility," after its nearly two decades of excessive materialism. The uncritical, "feel-good" mood of the eighties has been deflated by serious social problems. In some ways the nation's physical infrastructure may be seen as a fit (or "unfit") metaphor for the nation's social infrastructure. Just as bridges, sewer systems, and highways are in a shocking state of disrepair due to decades of neglect, so too is the condition of our inner cities, our children, our educational system, and our environment.

Sophisticated pollsters such as Lou Harris, Daniel Yankelovich, and the Roper Organization claim that there are clear indications that Americans are ready for the "tough appeals of self-sacrifice and discipline," and are willing to make public commitments to addressing such issues as drug abuse, poverty, pollution, and education reform. The strength of this commitment, however, is yet to be tested against the budgetary constraints of the next decade. Museums also will experience heightened pressures to be socially responsible. Increasingly, museums will be expected to justify their existence as vital community resources. Will women in turn have a special role in museums as social reformers once again? And will women be trapped in the position of nurturers or civilizers, or in fact occupy the most honorable of all museum roles?

EDUCATION

Museums must and will enhance their role in informal education. As we move from an industrial to an information economy, human capital has become the primary national concern, and knowledge has become our primary product. Ironically, as we enter into fierce competition with European and Asian trading blocs, we find that our educational system has failed to prepare our work force for a global economy. Compared to the children in most of the other developed countries, our young people score the lowest in academic achievement, leaving corporate America gravely concerned that it will not have workers fit for sophisticated service in high-technology industries. As efforts at school reform are made, society will increasingly look toward other institutions such as museums to supplement the formal learning of the largely overburdened classroom.

Museums can also benefit from the trend in education toward "lifelong learning." Education is no longer seen as a onetime accomplishment of certain "terminal" degrees facilitated in a formal learning environment. Instead, education is a process by which one is in a state of constant learning and "retooling," either for the ever-changing informational needs of the workplace or for the ever-changing expectations of personal growth.

Education departments must be trained to look past narrow definitions of education as "school programs." Educating the young remains critically important. One must remember, however, that by 2000, only 16 percent of Americans will be eighteen and under. That means museums should be very concerned with educating adults, who will make up 84 percent of the population. Not only will they be increasingly older but also either better educated or poorly educated. Twenty percent of adult Americans are illiterate.

It is also likely that educational reform will bring more attention to the controversial notion of "shared cultural knowledge," and its role in a pluralistic society. Museums should be further appreciated as repositories for this "core knowledge," at a time when information has become overwhelmingly complex and standards for excellence have become diffuse.

Museum education, however, has traditionally been a lower priority than collections acquisition and management within the museum establishment.

This lower status is indicated by the fact that museum education has long been ghettoized as "women's work". As education becomes the nation's number one priority, museum education must gain greater prestige. The importance of museum education will not be lost on the public. The broad local support increasingly needed by museums will likely be measured in how successfully a museum contributes to the informal education of the community's young people and adults, as well as to that of visitors in general—whether in arts, communications, or scientific and technical literacy. It is, therefore, likely that museum education experts will be indirectly responsible for the financial success of their institutions. Better collaboration with the schools, the local organizations, and the corporate community could assure financial support.

Museums, like other sectors of the economy such as the health-care industry, will have to move toward better "outcome measures." Survey research is still inadequate in museums. To justify their funding, museums increasingly will have to attempt to measure what visitors bring to a museum—their knowledge and their expectations—and what they take away—their satisfaction and their increased knowledge.

THE ENVIRONMENT

Value shifts toward social responsibility and the museum's heightened role as educator clearly converge when exploring such issues as the environment and health care. Some predict that with the apparent decline of political ideologies around the world, there will be one universal ideology that takes their place— global environmental responsibility. The nineties will see a growing urgency to solve massive environmental problems. Overpopulation, global warming, ozone depletion, and deforestation are now threatening a long-held assumption that the earth's natural resources are capable of sustaining human life. In 1900 the human population was 1.6 billion. By the summer of 1987 that figure was 5 billion and will surpass 6 billion by 2000. With a growth rate of 1 billion every twelve years, predictions for certain developing areas of the world are grim. Natural history, science, and technology museums, however, can now bring time, resources, and talent to bear on environmental problems. Through the use of multimedia, museums have the potential to educate the community well beyond the resources of the schools. For example, exhibits of "social relevance"—such as those depicting the role of rain forests in maintaining biological diversity, or illustrating alternative means of fuel production or waste remediation—will likely increase in the future. More socially relevant exhibits will also alleviate some of the bifurcation that Jean Weber mentions in her essay, "Changing Roles and Attitudes." She asks whether we can really justify taking money for cultural exhibits when those funds might be needed to address serious social problems. These issues do not have to be mutually exclusive.

The role of women is especially important in the human governance of the planet, because women will continue to have primary control over many of the activities that affect and are affected by the environment. In developing countries, for example, the women are largely responsible for family size, domestic agricultural production, and domestic consumption and sanitation. Museums can perform a great service by educating the public about women's important roles in environmental responsibility, which is an issue of women's universal plight. It also raises the question of the future of museums in developing nations. How quickly can museums leap from the preservation of high culture to education and social responsibility? Are many of our own museums even in a position to be teachers?

HEALTH CARE

Medical and health-care education is another area in which museums of the future can make greater contributions. We begin the decade with an ongoing health-care crisis. Nearly 12 percent of the gross national product provides roughly $500 billion in health care, leaving 37 million Americans without health insurance. Experts predict that by 2000 health-care costs could rise to 15 percent of the gross national product, or $1.5 trillion. A significant portion of these costs could be curbed through changes in behavior and lifestyle alone. The most significant shift in health care worldwide is the movement from treatment to health promotion and prevention. Health-promotion strategies of good diet, exercise, stress reduction, and avoidance of risk factors such as smoking and alcohol abuse need to be more effectively conveyed in museums.

Many health-care issues demand better health education. An AIDS epidemic that already has infected roughly 1.5 million Americans, rising rates of sexually transmitted diseases, drug abuse, crack babies, and an increasing number of children without immunization all call for extensive education programs to supplement those of struggling schools and churches. Furthermore, the nineties promise a more severe shortage of health-care providers, due partly to low salaries and low prestige, but also to the scientific and technical illiteracy that drives young people away from the sciences and the health-care professions. For example, it is estimated that there will be a shortage of

600,000 nurses by 2000, as well as a need for millions of more highly skilled technical workers.

In all aspects of health education—whether addressing women as potential providers or receivers of health care—the education of women is extremely important. For example, new scientific advancements in medicine, specifically biotechnology, will continue to present women with profound ethical choices. Research in gene mapping could make possible the diagnosis of more than four thousand genetic diseases. New reproductive technologies such as in vitro fertilization and surrogate motherhood are setting the stage for even more complicated choices regarding maternity, paternity, and the selection of the sex of one's child, and even its characteristics. On the distant horizon there will be the possibility of the ultimate demise of women's biological clock through hormonal therapy and frozen embryos. As a board member of the National Museum of Health and Medicine Foundation, I know that this range of health issues must be addressed in future museum exhibits.

I think that museums of the future must confront a host of ethical issues in order to maintain credibility with their public. Museums traditionally have been averse to taking risks and suspicious of "negative exhibits." Visitors, however, will increasingly demand interpretation as well as celebration of objects. Interpretation should mean confronting complex issues rather than simply celebrating society as we know it. The Holocaust Museum will break new ground by attempting to "entertain" with the most serious questions of all regarding genocide, the nature of evil, and an examination of modern progress.

INFORMATION TECHNOLOGY

Key to a museum's ability to meet the educational challenges that lie ahead will be its participation in the information revolution—a revolution that has only just begun. The next decade will bring awesome advances. Ninety percent of the work done today on mainframes will be performed by desktop computers by 2000, with only slight increases in cost. Erasable storage is likely, and data compression and other techniques may increase optical storage density by six times, whereby a compact disk could hold the equivalent of six thousand books. Phone systems will have end-to-end digital capability, carrying text, data, graphics, pictures, and full-motion video, as well as voice. Also available will be speaker-independent speech recognition systems that will recognize five thousand to fifteen thousand words of continuous speech.

Museums are already profoundly impacted by technologies. The Smithsonian's SELGEM and GRIPHOS data systems, designed to accommodate a large amount of information about objects in a museum, were installed nearly twenty years ago and are still in use. In the next decade, however, it is likely that the museum community will institute a national series of computer-based inventories of museum collections, along with an information-sharing system.

LEARNING TECHNOLOGIES

Museums will also feel the impact of advances in learning technologies and the "learning about learning" that is emerging from the neurosciences, the cognitive sciences, and other areas of the social sciences. Artificial intelligence techniques are being used to create intelligent tutoring systems that can diagnose defects in what a student understands, help students see the reasoning processes involved in solving problems, and respond to questions rather than always presenting information in a sequence predetermined by a programmer. Advanced computer simulations that use images, sounds, and text will lend realism to the curricular material and allow students to learn by following their own interests and blazing their own paths through large areas of knowledge. In hypermedia systems, users will be able to move easily through information in any form—text, data, sound, pictures, or video. By early next century, knowledge navigators or "knowbots" will help learners to find the exact "needles" of information they need within the vast "haystacks" of information available in electronic data bases.

With the introduction of hypermedia texts, museum computer inventories will not be bound to the printed word alone, but will offer tremendous capacity for image, color, sound, and categorization. For the first time, multisensory coding of art objects will be possible and will aid both museum staff and museum users. Sitting at a computer screen linked to an international network of museums and galleries, a user will be able to construct an individualized "museum without walls" by gathering together works of art or historical objects for the purpose of entertainment or analysis.

Insights from the cognitive sciences are especially intriguing for art museums. New theories of multiple intelligences have major implications for learning and teaching in the arts. Current education has been geared to linguistic/verbal and logico-mathematical intelligence, seldom allowing people to exercise spatial, kinesthetic, or musical intelligences. Stimulating interactive software that enables people to more fully appreciate the visual arts can be derived from these theories. So far it is children's museums that have most clearly addressed issues of the learning theory, as indicated in Ann Lewin's work at the Capital Children's Museum in Washington, D.C.

I call for museum women to possess what Mary Catherine Bateson has called "peripheral vision." Bateson says that in contrast to men, women don't go at anything, including their lives, in a linear way. They continually think around issues, raise tangential points, and consider possible implications traditionally overlooked. I would say then that museum women should be the "peripheral visionaries," the ones who have the power and confidence to ask new questions and to offer new interpretations, all the while keeping their eye on the prize—in this case, a preferred future for men, women, and the planet Earth.

NOTES

1. Elizabeth Cady Stanton, Susan B. Anthony, and Matilda Joslyn Gage, eds., *History of Woman Suffrage* (Rochester, N.Y.: Susan B. Anthony, 1887–1922).

2. Margaret Atwood, *The Handmaid's Tale* (Boston: Houghton Mifflin, 1986).

3. See Marvin J. Cetron, *American Renaissance: Our Life at the Turn of the 21st Century* (New York: St. Martin's Press, 1989); and John Naisbitt and Patricia Aburdene, *Megatrends 2000: Ten New Directions for the 1990s* (New York: Murrow, 1990).

Instituting Change

E. Kay Davis

HEATHER PAUL presents a thorough and penetrating analysis of the present and the future roles of women in our society and, more specifically, within the museum world. Both her concerns and aspirations are shared by women associated with museums. In her introductory comments, Paul is careful to use quotations to emphasize the extent to which women have historically been exploited in our society (and indeed, in all societies). In this respect, I first urge that professional women not fall into the trap that has plagued, for example, proponents of civil rights issues. The constant reiteration of the past wrongs committed by some segment of society often ultimately triggers a backlash from that sector, many of whose members are somewhat reluctant to respond to continuous, repetitive reminders of their past injustices and unjust attitudes. I suggest instead that today's women pursue a more understanding approach, based principally on the theme that modern women are both more capable than ever and are disposed toward more significant roles in the businesses of the world, because they have much to offer and are eager to serve. This approach displays no anger or rancor and has all the advantages of "motherhood and apple pie." Who can oppose a fervent, sincere desire to serve society?

As Paul points out concerning future demographics, museums of the next century must both recognize the extent to which elderly women and minorities are a major part of the museum public and respond accordingly. Not only should museums mirror the experiences of these groups, they should also utilize these groups as valuable resources that can contribute significantly to both the developmental and educational roles of museums.

In discussing the sexual politics of the workplace, I believe that using phrases such as "the authority and power of women in museum life" may suggest goals and aspirations among women that are not essentially nobly motivated. I prefer to imply that women are increasingly becoming directors, curators, and researchers in museums, because they are better prepared and have more to offer toward the success of museums. Although Paul states that museum education has long been "ghettoized as 'women's work,'" she then quickly notes that education is becoming a first priority of our society, so that the role of museum education will assume a more prestigious and financially important role within museums in the future. I do not consider it a "ghettoization" for women to have been relegated to educational roles in the past. Women recognized early what is only now being acknowledged more generally—that education is a primary and essential function of museums and is always of paramount service to society.

Paul carefully and thoughtfully considers and addresses environmental and health-care issues, as well as the challenges that museums face to educate the public about such issues. She correctly emphasizes the museums' role as public educator. Paul's concluding remarks relating to informational and learning technologies are especially appropriate for tomorrow's museums. The entire museum world must learn to keep abreast of the burgeoning technologies that will enhance our ability to learn and to understand the increasingly intricate information that we must provide for the public. Clearly, we must all be continuous learners as well as educators. Paul has clearly and forcefully reminded us not only of the tasks but also of the multitude of opportunities that lie ahead.

Learning from the Past

Tom Crouch

THE ANSWER to the basic question posed in these essays seems patently clear: Of course gender will make a difference. The real question is: How will the museum profession respond to inevitable social change? The answer seems to be compelling to many people. Perhaps this interest began with the controversy over the exhibition "Harlem on My Mind," at the Metropolitan Museum in New York. Since that time, over the past twenty years or so, the problems, the potential, and the very role of museums in our society have been the subject of heated public debate. Decisions made in the front offices and the boardrooms of the world's great museums—such as the Victoria and Albert Museum, the Corcoran Gallery of Art, and the New-York Historical Society—have become front-page news. Editorial writers wrestle with the question of whether the African American experience should be treated within a museum devoted to the broad sweep of American history or in a separate institution devoted solely to that topic. I heard a woman and a man debating the question of how appropriate Washington, D.C., is as the site for the Holocaust Museum. Even novelists are entering the debate. I do not think any of the readers of Tony Hillerman's *Talking God* are unaware of the author's opinion of museums' treatment of the physical remains and sacred objects of Native Americans.[1] The men and women who oversee our operations, the individuals and organizations that fund us, and the people who make up our audience are scrutinizing our attitudes and activities to an unprecedented degree. It is growing very hot indeed in certain corners of our collective kitchen. The result is that we have had to reexamine our goals for the future of our institutions. In this essay, I examine science and technology museums, using the museum at which I work, the National Air and Space Museum, as my prime example.

Congress established the National Air and Space Museum in 1946. Its charter directed the new museum to "memorialize the achievements of American men and women who have made pioneering contributions to aviation and space flight." Over the past forty-four years, I think the National Air and Space Museum has done a fairly good job of meeting that goal, which a worthy one. None of us would argue against the value of commemorating the achievements of the past. I do think, however, that we ought to be doing much more than that.

The 8.2 million visitors to the National Air and Space Museum in 1989 were citizens of a nation and a world that is shaped and dominated by the forces of science and technology, and most of the visitors are uncomfortable with that fact. Charles P. Snow was right all those years ago, when he argued in *The Two Cultures* that we find ourselves increasingly divided into two camps.[2] One includes those of us who understand the impact of science and technology on our lives and are willing and able to address the problems and the potential of technology in order to make personal decisions about it. The other group includes those who are willing to let their fellow citizens make such decisions for them. Despite our best efforts to deal with the business of two cultures, helping women and minorities to feel more comfortable in thinking about issues in science and technology remains a major problem. This is, of course, not solely a problem for women, but because of the cultural disadvantages women experience, it always seems that museums such as ours have a special obligation to empower women as much as possible in the science and technology fields. The need to do so is apparent.

How are we going to assist our visitors, who are already uncomfortable with and perhaps even frightened by the future and technology, to understand the importance of those forces in their lives? How can we make them more comfortable with the impact of scientific and technological change and better prepared to accept responsibility for making decisions about it? I think the answers, in part, are clear enough. Those of us who work in science and technology institutions need to redirect our thinking away from our own fascination with our disciplines, which is often a problem. We need to spend more time thinking about our audiences' needs and what we want to convey to them. Obviously, we want to provide them with information that will be useful in their lives. That information should be structured in a useful context. We have to be willing to say something worthwhile—perhaps even to take a chance once in a while.

Here is an example. For many years after its founding in the mid-sixties, the National Museum of American History was a fairly traditional place. Visitors saw machines lined up in chronological order—steam engines, scientific instruments, gasoline engines, and stagecoaches. We now find that sort of approach for exhibits problematical. The visitor who is already uncomfortable with the shiny, otherworldly quality of technology is not going to be a bit more comfortable when he or she sees things arranged in standard chronological pattern. This sends false messages to our visitors—no matter how comfortable they are with technology—because we are equating progress in technology and science with human progress, suggesting that every day and in every way we are getting better and better. If we are to assist Americans in addressing the problems of the future, we certainly have to move beyond the traditional approach and take chances.

We are already trying to do that. An exhibition at the National Museum of American History, "Science, Power, and Conflict," is an example of our efforts. When it was first introduced dichloro-diphenyl-trichloro-ethane (DDT) was hailed as a marvel of science, promising to revolutionize agricultural production, enabling us to grow enormous quantities of food. The exhibit traced the way in which early decisions about the safety and the long-term environmental impact of DDT were made, and focused on how subsequent research has called into question the wisdom of those early decisions. How do we decide what to do an what not to do? This exhibit demonstrates the direction in which we have to be willing to go. Is it dangerous? Sure it is—sometimes.

If we are to face the problems of assisting our visitors to understand our increasingly complex world, we have to be willing to displease some people. There are limits, but I think that we have to understand the need for balance. If we are to face the future with any hope for success in educating our visitors, honest presentations are an absolute requirement. I therefore disagree with the people who advocate the mere presentation of pure information in museums. To help visitors become more comfortable with science and technology, we have to accept the obligation to take a risk now and then, to present points of view. We have to let visitors know how the information we present fits into social patterns. We have to admit that science and technology are social phenomena, about which visitors can and should be making decisions.

NOTES

1. See Tony Hillerman, *Talking God* (New York: Harper and Row, 1989).
2. See Charles P. Snow, *The Two Cultures* (Cambridge, England: Cambridge University Press, 1959).

Assuming Leadership Roles

Christina Orr-Cahall

I AM very pleased that the futurists are looking at museums. Heather Paul's "In Preparation for the Future" and John Naisbitt's *Megatrends 2000* both suggest that the future will be our moment to excel. (The first *Megatrends* had not a word about museums, or arts at all.) Museums will become more businesslike than they have been in the past. Most of us are still trying to get the thunder of the last decade out of our ears, as we have already become more business oriented with shops that sometimes seem to be the primary purpose of museums' existence. Some contributors to this volume say that museums are becoming more global, which is an interesting and probably valid assessment. Tom Krens, the director of the Guggenheim, is setting up Guggenheim satellite museums around the world. Educated in both art history and business, Krens is in the forefront of what the futurists believe will happen.

The issue of entrepreneurship certainly becomes important if we are to operate and to finance museums in the traditional business manner. Women are good at entrepreneurship, because traditionally they have had to be. They are risk takers and have entrepreneurial instincts, both of which are characteristics that will enable them to excel at their work and to make substantial contributions to museums of the future. Museums have been befuddled by their rapid growth and by economic and societal changes. Leadership in museums is going to be crucial. It must work toward achieving consensus and bringing people together, which is something that women do well.

At an art museum directors conference, I attended a discussion given by David Carnes, an audience development researcher from Dayton, Ohio, who had studied the Dayton Museum. He discussed extensively the baby boomers, people born between 1946 and 1963, which is my generation by one year. They are a tough group of people, the type that gets involved and looks at the product. For example, they examine how the organization is run, before they decide whether or not to get involved with it, whether joining as a member, participating as a volunteer, or joining as staff. The baby boomers are the people that museums are counting on for financial support. They are going to be difficult to reach. Carnes believes that museum marketing must shift its focus from increasing attendance to supplying quality services. Museums will need solid, professional program development in order to win over the baby boomers, and to make them, as important contributors to the society that they care about, choose and believe in our cultural organizations.

There are things I foresee that we should be thinking about as indexes for the future. First, I believe we are going to see a more sophisticated level of volunteerism. Baby boomers will retire at a younger age and make up a significant segment of the population. If institutions are able to interest them, then baby boomers as staff or volunteers will be able to supply these institutions with professional skills that may not otherwise be available. Museums should plan with that in mind. It will take a decade or two of reconceptualizing the role of volunteers before museums are able to incorporate that.

Second, I think museums are going to be linked fundamentally to the educational system at all levels—from the university, to continuing education, to kindergarten. Many museums have not yet established this connection—at least they have not done it well. They tend to give parties or to present exhibitions or lectures and expect the schools to come. There must, however, be a more substantial incorporation of the educational system into museums.

Government should be involved as well. For example, an institution's trustees or its director can talk to the governor of the state. At a recent conference on education, the governors expressed strong views. The questions become: How will we play a role in government educational policy making—not what role will they play for us?

Museums and other groups have to start working in unison, not in competition. I am tired of people competing against each other in the world of culture. Museum professionals have to align themselves to their cultural institutions, as well as those in competition with them.

Futurists must acknowledge that there will be less emphasis on the real tangible object, because objects will be placed in their sociocultural contexts. In my work, I have always done this. I am against, however, providing the public with access to objects through a medium with which they would not have to go to the museum. They should still have to see the object. I suspect I will have to forget that notion, and soon. This principle of indirect contact with the object functions easiest in the performing arts, where, for example, an audience can watch an opera on television. Some museum professionals tell us: "Don't even bother to put out the real objects. It's so damaging to them. Why are you doing that anyway?" The British Conservancy Board is the primary leader of this approach. The questions become: Does the museum need this object? If so, how can the museum translate it into the new technology and continue to attract people to the museum? Is it enough for people to learn through another technological process? What is it that the museum is trying to do? Is the museum trying to ingratiate itself by having people visit and see the objects, or is it trying to teach the public by other means to raise their interest in these objects?

There are some pragmatical steps we, as museum professionals, can take. First, assuming that we want to advance in this field, we should educate ourselves in entrepreneurship and in technology, taking the extra course, reading the books, talking to our colleagues, and asking questions. When I was in a Ph.D. program in art history at Yale University, I told the administrators that I wanted to get an M.B.A. They said that that was absolutely absurd, because someone with a Yale degree does not need an M.B.A. I wish I had gotten one. Second, we should become more politically and technologically savvy. Doing so is crucial, if we are to succeed in the next decade without being directed by others but by ourselves. We must also demand our rights. For example, at the Corcoran Gallery of Art the employees completed the first human resources survey ever conducted at the institution. The survey results indicated that the majority of the staff believed that the most important issue was a pay increase for the lower-level staff. Next, we must each recognize what we do well and do it. Many of us feel that there is something wonderful about being a director and subliminally aim to become one. We should determine where we can make the best contribution, because at the end of our careers, that is where we want to be. The titles ultimately will not matter, but it is too easy to believe that they will.

We need to tell our colleagues when their job performance is good, which we forget to do. We often fail to acknowledge our colleagues' successes, tending only to remember something they did that we did not like. If we tell somebody when they do well, they will tell us when we do well, and we will learn from that. Such an attitude will promote a better work environment, contributing to the development of an environment in which a consensus can be reached, rather than one in which competitiveness thrives. This should be the ultimate goal of leadership and management.

Furthermore, we should be involved with mentorships. I believe that people foster other people in the art world, and whom one knows is still a factor in one's career development. I have been lucky to have had many good mentors, and in the past year, many of them have aided me. Their help was greatly appreciated. You may think, "Who could I be a mentor to?" You could be a mentor to an intern. You could be a mentor to a person who wants to reenter the workplace. I have always advocated employing women returning to the workplace, although there is considerable opposition. In the two years that I worked at the Corcoran Gallery of Art, the museum hired for professional positions two women who had not worked in the last twenty years. The museum did the same with several minorities who had not really held significant positions in the institution.

Can we be all things to all people? No. But what we can do is represent more people. In this way, we will be more to more people.

PART 7

Theory in Practice

About an Exhibition

AN INNOVATIVE approach to gender differences in an exhibition is discussed in the following essay by Barbara Clark Smith. She describes the research and the planning that were required—as well as the problems that were encountered—before, during, and after the planning and the production of the exhibition "Men and Women: A History of Costume, Gender, and Power," at the National Museum of American History. This case study of applied feminist theories asks: When we think "public," do we think "male"? How do women become the center of the mainstream? What matters most about an object, a description, or a role? Smith also shows how she managed in the exhibition to treat historical relationships between social rules for male and female appearance on the one hand, and the gender roles prescribed for men and women on the other hand. Smith brought to the project a background in social history and a self-aware feminism that knit costume history with larger issues.

Jane R. Glaser and Artemis A. Zenetou

A Case Study of Applied Feminist Theories

Barbara Clark Smith

THREE PRINCIPAL thoughts about women and museums evolved from my work on the exhibition, "Men and Women: A History of Costume, Gender, and Power," at the National Museum of American History. Several of these tenets were imperfectly expressed in the exhibition, for they represent not so much what I brought to the exhibition as what I have taken from it. In this essay I discuss three interrelated topics: the audience we address, the artifacts we interpret, and the subjects that we choose to teach.

In the midst of working on "Men and Women," I realized that I was only addressing women as my audience, excluding men from my imaginative construction of museum visitors. Indeed, I came to the conviction that my best work, my strongest thinking and writing, came when I constructed my audience in this way. Like other curators, I began the project with numerous questions about the public: What does my audience care about? What do they need to know? What language or languages will make sense and prove accessible to them? Perhaps because the exhibition treats relationships of gender and power in American society, I realized that I needed to confront questions about the gender and the power of the audience. I had to consider that my topic might cause controversy or give offense, a prospect that in a variety of ways had already impeded the exhibition's progress. I found that I could think most clearly about my audience's needs when I was not worrying about offending men but focusing instead on informing and engaging women. In part, I had discovered the energy that comes from a positive standpoint rather than a negative one. It was constricting to wonder, "What should I avoid?" or "What am I obligated to do?" It felt expansive to ask: "What is this an opportunity to accomplish or, at least, to attempt?" To reach this positive frame, I found it vital to place women museum visitors fully at center stage.

I confess that it took some nerve for me to acknowledge that I was willing to limit my thinking—and hence my responsibility—according to lines of gender. I even hesitate to acknowledge it here. After all, is not such an approach partial and limiting rather than enhancing? Do I not have an obligation to address the whole public?

Despite these doubts, I was reassured by several reflections. Six million visitors attend the National Museum of American History every year, and roughly half of them are women. Three million is not a paltry audience. People may protest against the exclusivity of the concept behind "Men and Women," but they rarely express doubts about the universal attraction of exhibitions on steam engines, duck stamps, or atomic clocks. Universal appeal is, after all, a chimera, and it is, tellingly, a requirement rarely brought to exhibitions that promise to interest a segment of the male population. Moreover, I have colleagues dedicated—in practice, if not explicitly—to speaking only to an audience of men in their work. Taken as a whole, the Museum of American History's exhibitions are neither gender neutral nor objective. I reassured myself with the awareness that one small, temporary exhibition addressed to women would not tip the scales in favor of feminism.

Equally important are the fundamental problems that underlie the concept of "the public," which informs much of our work in museums. To begin with, that "public" remains intangible. Although I have heard authoritative statements about what "the visitor" wants to know, needs to learn first, or will be willing to give attention to, I am not convinced that anyone has a good idea of these things. I know that thoughtful and intelligent people have begun the crucial task of learning about and from museum audiences. Yet we museum professionals often remain largely ignorant, promoting our own interests and concerns, all under cover of concern for the public and its supposed needs and limitations.

Opening ourselves to museum audiences strikes me as one of our primary challenges at this moment in museum work. Yet this challenge will not be met simply by circulating more questionnaires among museumgoers. I am troubled by the fact that many of the methods we have for investigating and gathering our public's ideas, interests, or responses have been devised by agencies that approach people not as an audience but as a market. Their concerns are not about education but sales. Their techniques produce "data" that they claim to be neutral—"information," nothing more and nothing less. As a feminist, I am skeptical about claims of objectivity and leery about the alleged dissociation of means and ends. I do not believe that museum professionals can expect such techniques to introduce museums to a process of creative thought and interaction. In this context it is up to us as feminists to reframe the matter—to reject the patina of "objectivity," to think more deeply about how we might listen to and engage our audiences. We have to do what these techniques generally do not do: inform, question, rankle, prod, and invite visitors not merely to answer our questions but also to speak actively to and with us.

One other consideration is relevant to the ways in which we approach and define our public. "Public" is a historical construct, one that, although it presents itself as all-encompassing and universal, has often been exclusively male. Over a decade ago, historian Joan Kelly noted that the Renaissance, hailed as an era of great public learning, was not such an era for European women.[1] Also, Joan Landes has argued that the broad public realm opened by the revolutions of the late eighteenth century empowered many men but explicitly excluded women.[2] Today women still play a role unequal to that of men in the public debate and the decision making about the public weal. We undoubtedly live with the legacy of this history of female exclusion today, because when we think about the public, we often think male.

Indeed, I have felt this, in my own life and in my thinking, as a concern for convincing men, meeting men's eyes in mixed gatherings, and investing power in men's responses to my ideas, as well as in their opinions and conclusions. Every woman has experienced sitting in a classroom or conference room and not really being spoken to (not just by male colleagues but also by other women). This not merely a remnant of the speaker's sexist upbringing but also an index of male power. In such situations, it is often most effective for women to convince men of their point of view, because men can often sway others, since they are objectively and observably in positions of influence and authority. In so much of our experience and in so many of our institutions, men are the professors, the supervisors, the bosses, and the "board." Even when these men exhibit sympathy and integrity, our long training and long practice at shaping our thoughts to their ears can still block our insights, interrupt our conversations, and deflect our thought processes. It is not surprising then that we might be able to take that thought process further in a universe imaginatively constructed to be female. Given this context, if I limit my audience to women, then I may have in fact deepened it.

I suggest we need to go further, to be not less but more specific in our thinking about museum visitors. I am European American and middle-class, and I am consciously struggling to be aware of ways that "woman" evokes in my mind an image of someone like myself. If we all, however, imagine our audience to be women of color, lesbian women, women with disabilities, working-class women, and poor women, then what does this do to our thinking about our exhibitions? It does not seem adequate for the goal to be *including* these women; instead, we (meaning all of these women, as well as myself) need to make them the central participants. I am struggling toward a new way of thinking and feeling about museum visitors, a reformulation in which they are not so much audience as they are sister discussants. In a feminist framework a curator might step beyond a posture of "including" her sisters in the audience; a curator might instead include herself in the investigation and the discussion of the experiences that arise from their world.

While working on "Men and Women," I felt unable to fully achieve this goal, in part, because the project I inherited had excluded class and color considerations, and, in part, because the reformulation I advocate requires such an extensive changing of perspective of everyone involved in producing an exhibition. My institution (myself included), in other words, is only a few steps of the way there. In this no doubt common situation it seemed essential not merely to add attention to women and people of color where possible but also to eschew claims of universal representation at every point. This we must do in our label text but also in more visual and innovative ways. When our exhibitions treat elite or middle-class white Americans, we must be sure to locate them as such, depicting them as they were influenced by their class and racial position, and taking account of the agency of the other Americans who made their aspirations felt in our subjects' lives.

Overall, I think our goal should be to put aside the supposed obligation to start in the middle or the mainstream, adding the perspectives of women, people of color, working people, or lesbians and gays. The crucial question is: Where *is* the middle? The power to answer that—to assume centrality for oneself and then liberally to decide to include others—represents the fundamental power to define the basic narrative of American history, which sets boundaries to our imaginations and determines what is at stake. Surely women who work in museums and those who attend museum programs and exhibitions need to be responsible for placing ourselves, our questions, and our experiences at the center. One women's issue that we would then open for ourselves and our visitors is the question of how museums—how any of our society's institutions—locate "the center."

To do this, to take sides, to locate ourselves, and to be partial in a self-conscious way is more responsible and respectful toward any museumgoer than to pretend to an inclusiveness and universality that we have done nothing to earn. If challenged on this stance, I would argue that this approach is not so exclusive as it might first seem, and that it might serve men who visit our exhibitions as well as women. Much of my education consisted of listening to male conversations as they took place in the classroom and in the texts and events expounded there. How Aristotle departed from Plato, what Stalin said to Churchill, and how Emerson engaged with Thoreau—these and like topics consumed my class time. Scholarly fields ranging from history to philosophy to science, literature, and law have developed through the medium of male conversation. If I have benefitted from this listening, might not men who visit the National Museum of American History learn from listening to a conversation among women?

In refusing to engage a male audience, I hope it is clear that it is far from my purpose to offend men; however, it is not my priority to avoid doing so. Offending someone is not the worst thing you can do to him or her. Perhaps we are less respectful to our visitors when we waste their time and belittle rather than challenge their capacities, presenting them with the reassuringly familiar instead of with questions, observations, and insights that are the product of our own hard work and hard thinking.

ARTIFACTS

This way of framing an audience leads us to a different approach to artifacts in our collections. As is so often the case, feminism asks us to look again, to see things anew. Some years ago I began work on an exhibition that included three case studies of eighteenth-century individuals. I noted the lack of attention to women's history, and proposed changing one of the case studies so that it focused on a woman rather than a man. One reply was that this was a laudable aim, but that there were no artifacts available pertaining to women. This exhibition, however, included period rooms and furnishings, pots, pans, toys, spinning wheels, costume and jewelry, artisan tools, and ceramic wares! This incident reflects not an idiosyncratic blindness, but a common one shared among many museum professionals and among many visitors who have their own experiences and who are a product of an invidiously gendered society that has been blind to women and their lives.

With our awareness of this common blindness, we need to look again at the objects in our collections and to think again about how we present them to our audiences. The consequences of remedying this blindness will certainly go far beyond but also will include a number of approaches. First, we will reject the approach favored by many curators of "letting the objects speak for themselves," not burdening them with interpretation—whether in the form of label text, juxtaposition with other objects, or innovative design techniques. We need active interpreters, because without such intervention, our audiences are apt to see what they have been taught to see and to remain blind to what they have been taught to ignore. For many of us an array of spinning jennies will more readily suggest a story of technological innovation and industrial progress than it will evoke images of women and children workers. We thus need to intervene in order to "people" that array—to give it context and meaning. We need labeling, design, and imaginative collaboration to devise ways to show visitors how jennies spun connections among classes, genders, races, and regions in America. It is incumbent on us, as we work toward revision, not to leave our visitors where they were when they entered the museum.

Second, the goal of taking a female audience seriously puts us strongly on the side of social and cultural history. I contest the claim that the material of which an object is made—metal, plastic, wood, fabric, paper—is more basic to its nature than the social and cultural meanings that men and women have given that object. In turn, to focus on those meanings requires us to rethink many of our conventions in object labeling. This means going through every gallery to remove sexism from labeling. An example is labels that call John Adams "Adams" and Abigail Adams "Abigail." I also cite as an example the companion portraits labeled as "Helen Caldicott (Mrs. William Penn)" and "William Penn," where the second label is unmodified by reference to the spouse. Additionally, I refer to the conventions inherited from fields such as decorative arts and costume history. In "Men and Women" the designer and I spent time considering our object labels: Is the maker of this suit of clothes important, as well as the date on which it was made, the fabric, and the provenance? If so, why? In the eyes of many costume historians, the answers to these questions constitute basic knowledge of the object. We decided to minimize much of this information to focus instead on identifying clothes by gender and class, as well as by time period. What matters about an object? Other people's answers will differ from mine; we need, however, to open the questions for discussion.

Finally, making women visitors central will lead us to reexamine the voice we should use when we write label text and design for exhibitions. Should we adopt a voice of authority? Should we use that voice—or any one voice—exclusively? The answers to these questions are not self-evident. Feminism questions authority; however, we must hesitate to jettison an authoritative voice just at the moment when we have reached positions from which we might use it. In "Men and Women" I encountered a further problem of language associated with the conventions of the particular field of costume history, a field that has validated itself in part by devising an objective—and sometimes objectifying—language for describing the allegedly trivial and certainly dangerous topic of clothing and its relation to human bodies. For example, did corsets of the 1840s constrict women's waists and push their flesh "upward," or did they constrict women's waists and make them look more busty? The language we use matters, because it can clarify or obscure our perspective, or distance or engage a reader. The voice itself can tell visitors, "Here is a distant, significant historical subject," or, "Here. This is about your body, your experience, your life." We need to worry and to argue over our language in every project we undertake in order to look at the conventions anew.

Most important, we must recognize that each convention of the museum world is not neutral but pointed, arising from a "professionalism" often constructed as a male conversation. Adapting to the conventions can represent a decision to confirm our visitors in the errors embodied in biased and sex-specific points of view. From a free, frank interpretive stance—a feminist one—we will develop a willingness to make our own decisions as to what is important for people to know. I would argue that one of the most fundamental questions that we must raise about our artifacts is: What is their role and where do they fit in a society that is profoundly gendered, that systematically discriminates against women, and that offers differential access to education and to economic, political, and cultural power? This question does not arise from an abstract commitment to gender issues but is grounded in much of the best historical work of this generation. Gender issues stand, along with race and class issues, at the heart of our past. It follows that we need to locate our artifacts in an authentic history that takes full account of this.

SUBJECTS FOR AN EXHIBITION

Taking women as our audience and casting our museum artifacts into the gendered societies that have produced, used, marketed, consumed, collected, and displayed them amounts to producing exhibitions about power relations between men and women. That is what "Men and Women" was about; its private title in my mind has long been "Who Wears the Pants?" I hope it is clear that I am not encouraging anyone to replicate this exhibition but suggesting something more far-reaching. Gender studies provides a methodology not just for a single exhibition but for *every* one, offering ways of analyzing and knowing not just some museum objects, but *all*.

This belief encourages us to continue the process we have started—doing different exhibitions, tackling topics that seem crucial to us, redressing the male bias of what our museums include and exclude. All of us who work in "technology" museums, for example, might lobby our institutions to deal responsibly with the technology so significant—both by its presence and its politically determined absence—in many women's lives: birth control. As we add new topics to our institutions, moreover, we can also change the exhibitions and programs that we retain, because most of these are deeply biased. For example, I would ask of the Smithsonian's National Air and Space Museum not that they add more information about Amelia Earhart and Sally Ride, or that they expand their stewardess uniform collection, but that they reinterpret their whole enterprise, questioning its basis. Surely a vital question about the airplanes, rockets, and other artifacts in the museum revolves around the extent to which they have been created by and for men. How are they expressive of a particular, historically male imagination? Why has access to these technologies and command over these tools been so limited, and what have been the consequences? What does this gendering mean for our understanding of "man's love for flight" or his quest to build bigger, better, faster, and indeed, evermore destructive aircraft? What have the relationships been among the exclusion of women, the limitation of flight to men of a particular class and race, and the uses of American airplanes to bomb civilian populations that are so often composed of people of color? How are we to understand space exploration, which is most symbolic in that ever-so-male gesture of planting a flag on the moon, claiming it as one's own on behalf of the nation-state? That gesture has historical significance, and it is women and people of color who are in a position to interpret what it has meant when privileged European and European American men have made that gesture. These are the sorts of questions that a feminist would have the National Air and Space Museum address.

At the National Museum of American History there is the question of the gowns in First Ladies Hall. I would choose to remove them from public view in order to use the precious museum space for other, more pressing needs. The gowns, however, are popular. Apparently, not that many museum professionals and visitors seem to be offended by such an exhibit that casts women principally in terms of their relationship to men. Given that, we might retain the gowns but raise the central questions directly. What does our abiding interest in these gowns mean? Why do these gowns seem to twentieth-century Americans to represent something that matters about these women? Why this insistence on their bodies, and how does this fit into a culture that defines women's bodies as objects of consumption, observation, and public view? Why this attention to their efforts at self-decoration rather than to their other aspirations or accomplishments? Exhibition of the first ladies' dresses speaks to and about a form of prominence, about one route open to women who have been included in history through their connection with a powerful man. If we are not to reinforce the idea that it is natural that women's importance be measured this way, then we need to lay bare the peculiar underlying premises of this long-standing and popular exhibition. We need to raise the questions of what it is precisely that makes these gowns popular and why they appear as they do at the National Museum of American History.

In my discussion of female audience and feminist approaches to artifacts and the framing of exhibition topics. I hope that it is clear that I mean something other than eliding the history and experience of men. ("Men and Women," as its title suggests, grapples with men's history and men's experience as well as women's!) It seems crucial that women's impact on museums not be limited to treating women's history and women's artifacts, but also include locating men's history and men's artifacts in their partial and gendered context. To that end, I want to suggest that it is less relevant to examine "the impact of women on museums" than it is to examine the impact of men or, more honestly and accurately, the impact of masculinism. For it is not the biological male that shapes these institutions, but rather the ideology of masculinism, a point of view that privileges men's experiences, aspirations, and perspectives, not only imagining these to be most important but also believing them to be most representative of all. We are slowly countering these most basic of assumptions: that the male gaze is objective, that men's ideals constitute "the truly human," that a "museum of man" is inclusive, and that it can be our highest aspiration to seek the "increase and diffusion of knowledge among men."

We should not underestimate or fear to acknowledge to one another the difficulty and the radicalism of our objectives. If we are rethinking history, art, or science, we are creating a way of knowing that proceeds not only from women's experience but also, surprisingly, from men's in a gendered world. To accomplish this, to claim it forthrightly as our purpose, is to change ourselves and our thinking through our work together. This recognition does nothing so much as it underscores our need to talk with one another, to examine constantly with one another the institutions in which we are working and that we need to transform. As we continue organizing and exploring among ourselves, we might consider that perhaps we take our strongest stand vis-à-vis those institutions by affirming and deepening our connections with communities of women outside this profession.

NOTES

1. Joan Kelly, "The Social Relation of the Sexes: Methodological Implication of Women's History," *Signs* 1, no. 4 (Summer 1976).

2. See Joan B. Landes, *Women and the Public Sphere in the Age of the French Revolution* (Ithaca: Cornell University Press, 1988).

PART 8

Conclusion

Toward a Collective Perspective

WHAT ARE the next steps? Where do we go from here? This is both an intellectual process and one that requires plans for action. What should we be doing together and individually? Who are we as women in the museum world?

The preceding essays show that we agree on much but are also beginning to disagree, which is an important sign of a rich and healthy approach to the issues that we are facing. I believe that we have the power and the confidence to be the peripheral visionaries of the future—for women, for men, and for the planet.

Kathy Dwyer Southern

Summary and Calls to Action

Susan Stitt

THE CONTRIBUTORS to this volume focus on many views of gender issues in museums. Having absorbed all of these different outlooks—their strengths and varieties of values relating to gender in our small yet broad field—I will offer some summary statements.

Women's issues and concerns are not easily summarized, and it is presumptuous, in the wake of so many ways of looking at the topic, to do so. First, I will endeavor to establish the right or the authority to summarize. Second, I will connect the contributors' themes and suggest some closing statements, if not conclusions, and calls to action.

In 1975 I was on the first American Association for State and Local History panel that explored the status of women in museums. During this period the American Association of Museums (AAM) had a Women's Caucus, of which I was its second president. More so than the caucus itself, its expression of concern was the vehicle through which issues of the sixties slowly entered the museum field. One of our goals was to advocate more women in the national office of the AAM, because there were almost none. We also sought to sponsor sessions at the association's annual meeting in order to give more visibility to women in the field, as well as to women's issues. By the mid-seventies we thought those goals were accomplished. The caucus was dissolved.

My 1975 *Museum News* article on the status of women in museums, which cited statistical data on the number of women employed in various capacities in museums nationwide—their age, experience, education, and salary—provided the first hard statistics on the status—based on titles and salaries—of women in our field.[1] By the time that article was published (my tenth anniversary in the field), I had worked in four different museums—as a first woman director, a first woman administrator, a first woman grants coordinator, and a woman special project director. In that decade I was involved in two lawsuits. The first incident involved straightforward sexual discrimination. As I read the accreditation application from the director, I discovered that the men, not the women, on staff got pensions. The other incident involved a breach of contract, in which I was vulnerable because I was female. Neither case went to court; I won one and lost the other on a technicality. I was not overly conscious of women's issues when I designed the national surveys that resulted in the article that publicized that the salaries of museum women were about 30 percent less than those of museum men.

There is a story to tell about my taking charge of my life and freeing myself from the prison of what Mary Schmidt Campbell describes as the "superwomen myth." In December 1989 I was appointed president of the Historical Society of Pennsylvania. This appointment marked my coming full circle professionally, because in 1966—my first year in the museum field—I served as assistant to the director of this society. Two dozen years later I was invited to return as director, and I am now president. It is interesting that even though I am the society's first woman chief executive since its founding in 1824, no one has noticed that fact—not the trustees, the staff, or the press. It is as though the questions I have asked during my career about why women were treated differently in this field had all been answered. My gender is not an issue—at least not at the Historical Society of Pennsylvania. In general, however, gender is an issue, and defining it occupies our attention.

Individual achievements have been a theme in these essays. The intellectual framework for the interplay of individualism and community is introduced by Campbell. Lois W. Banner elaborates on this theme in "Three Stages of Development," which describes the three-stage process of feminist scholarship over the past twenty years. It is fascinating to observe how all the contributors represent one or more of these stages and are in different stages in the development of their feminism.

A second theme in the essays is the feminist perspective, or "angle of vision," as Edith P. Mayo describes it in "New Angles of Vision." I appreciate her effort to define this perspective, which was seen by others as enriching all areas of the museum. My perspective was also broadened and my consciousness was raised by Barbara Clark Smith's essay, in which she describes her thought process in developing the exhibition "Men and Women: A History of Costume, Gender, and Power." Is what we call feminism actually humanism? Will the third stage, the integrative stage of the women's movement, be the practicing of humanism?

A third theme has been the concept of empowerment of women, African Americans, children, and other groups by their representation in museums. Whether museums are politically strong in relation to empowerment is a question on which not all essayists agree.

In addition to the themes and observations that the contributors explore, there are also some interesting omissions. Money, or the lack of it, was not a major point of discussion. In his presentation at the symposium, Frank Talbot noted the "high cost of change." Mayo mentions the impact of funding upon exhibition perspective, and vice versa. Money as a problem and as a solution is addressed by the essayists. It is interesting, however, to observe that they do not think of throwing money at the problem as the only solution or even perhaps as a useful answer to gender problems. The essayists also provide little specific documentation of discriminatory problems in the museum field. Are we past that first stage of documenting discrimination?

Responsible commitment to women's rights in our field should be more fully discussed. Such commitment involves the obligation to mentor. In her presentation at the conference, Marcia Tucker remarked that "when you get older, people sometimes listen to what you have to say." This suggests that speaking out on women's issues and on other issues is a duty for those with seniority. Years of service also bring with them the responsibility to serve as mentors for younger women and to enhance their involvement in the field. Those fortunate enough to be seniors also have a responsibility to the oral tradition. Perhaps because it is a small field, or perhaps for more complex reasons, the museum field has little shared memory.

Consciousness-raising is not a onetime experience. Sensitivity to the multiple levels and nuances of discrimination should be widespread. We have a personal responsibility as well as a duty to others to expose ourselves to concerns and to expressions of insight from others.

What are the conclusions? Is there an action plan emerging? Yes, broadly described, the first mandate on that plan is to bear witness. Robert Sullivan in "Evaluating the Ethics and Consciences of Museums" presents a list of ways to begin immediately to address these issues. The second mandate is the responsibility to be a mentor. And the third implied duty is for women to be themselves, with all the diversity and depth available, and not try to be superwomen.

This is a concise action plan, but a powerful one.

NOTE

1. Susan Stitt, "The Search for Equality," *Museum News* 54 (September-October 1975): 17–23

Selected Bibliography

This selected bibliography has been prepared to aid the reader in locating material on the impact of gender perspectives in scholarship, education, and communication, particularly as it relates to the museum environment. Included are journal articles and books from the fine arts, museum studies, history, psychology, and women's studies.

Abbe, Mary. "Kathy Halbreich: 'Popular without Pandering.'" *Artnews* 90 (January 1991): 85–86.

Anderson, Margaret, and Kylie Winkworth. "Museum and Gender: An Australian Critique." *Museum* 171 (1991): 147–51.

Birke, Lynda. *Women, Feminism, and Biology: The Feminist Challenge*. Brighton, England: Wheatsheaf Press, 1986.

Braz Texeira, Madalena. "From Strength to Strength: A Short History of Museums and Women in Portugal." *Museum* 171 (1991): 126–28.

Broude, Norma, and Mary D. Garrard. "Feminist Art History and the Academy: Where Are We Now?" *Women's Studies Quarterly* 15 (Spring-Summer 1987): 10–16.

Campbell, Mary Schmidt. "Beyond Individuals." *Museum News* 69 (July-August 1990): 37–40.

"A Citizen of the World: The Museum Profession Honors Grace McCann Morley." *Museum News* 63 (February 1985): 37–41.

Cummins, Alissandra. "The Role of Women in Caribbean Museum Development: Where Are We Now?" *Museum* 171 (1991): 140–43.

de Lauretis, Teresa, ed. *Feminist Studies/Critical Studies.* Bloomington: Indiana University Press, 1986.

des Portes, Elisabeth, and Anne Raffin. "Women in ICOM." *Museum* 171 (1991): 129–32.

Diamond, Irene, and Lee Quimby, eds. *Feminism and Foucault: Reflections on Resistance.* Boston: Northeastern University Press, 1988.

Differences: A Journal of Feminist Cultural Studies 1 (Summer 1989). Theme issue: "The Essential Difference: Another Look at Essentialism."

DuBois, Ellen Carol, Gail Paradise Kelly, Elizabeth Lapovsky Kennedy, Carolyn W. Korsmeyer, and Lillian S. Robinson. *Feminist Scholarship: Kindling in the Groves of Academe.* Urbana: University of Illinois Press, 1985.

Faludi, Susan. *Backlash: The Undeclared War against American Women.* New York: Crown, 1991.

Frisch, Michael H. "The Memory of History." In *Presenting the Past: Essays on History and the Public,* eds. Susan Porter Benson, Stephen Brier, and Roy Rosenzweig, 5–17. Philadelphia: Temple University Press, 1986.

From Women's Eyes. Exhibition catalog. Waltham, Mass.: Rose Art Museum, Brandeis University, 1977.

Gallop, Jane. *Reading Lacan.* Ithaca, N.Y.: Cornell University Press, 1985.

Gangewere, R. Jay. "Talking to Marsha Bol." *Carnegie Magazine* 60 (May-June 1991): 30–35, 38.

Garrard, Mary D. "'Of Men, Women, and Art': Some Historical Reflections." In *Feminist Collage: Educating Women in the Visual Arts,* ed. Judy Loeb, 138–55. New York: Teachers College Press, 1979.

Glaser, Jane R. "The Impact of Women on Museums: An American Seminar." *Museum* 171 (1991): 180–82

Glueck, Grace. "Making Cultural Institutions More Responsive to Social Needs." *Arts in Society* 11 (Spring-Summer 1974): 48–54.

Gouma-Peterson, Thalia and Patricia Mathews. "The Feminist Critique of Art History." *Art Bulletin* 69 (September 1987): 326–57.

Grab, Titus. "'Women's Concerns Are Men's Concerns': Gender Roles in German Museums." *Museum* 171 (1991): 136–39.

Harris, Ann Sutherland. "Women in College Art Departments and Museums." *Art Journal* 32 (Summer 1973): 417–19.

Harvey, Kerridwen. *Engendering Change: The Research and Exhibition of Contemporary Women's Issues in the Museum.* Toronto: University of Toronto, 1992.

Heartney, Eleanor. "How Wide Is the Gender Gap?" *Artnews* 86 (Summer 1987): 139–45.

Herreman, Yani. "Some Facts and Myths in Mexico." *Museum* 171 (1991): 133–35.

Howe, Barbara J., and Emory L. Kemp, eds. *Public History: An Introduction.* Malabar, Fla.: Robert E. Krieger Publishing, 1986.

Jones, Sian. "The Female Perspective." *Museums Journal* 91 (February 1991): 24–27.

Justice, Betty, and Renate Pore, eds. *Toward the Second Decade: The Impact of the Women's Movement on American Institutions.* Westport, Conn.: Greenwood Press, 1981.

Kaplan, Flora. "Nigeria: Shedding a Ghostly Presence." *Museum* 171 (1991): 163–66.

Karp, Ivan, and Steven D. Lavine, eds. *Exhibiting Cultures: The Poetics and Politics of Museum Display.* Washington, D.C.: Smithsonian Institution Press, 1991.

Keller, Evelyn Fox. *Reflections on Gender and Science.* New Haven: Yale University Press, 1985.

Kelly, Joan. *Women, History and Theory: The Essays of Joan Kelly.* Chicago: University of Chicago Press, 1984.

Kirby, Sue, and Jane Legget. "WHAM Weekend." *Museums Journal* 90 (October 1990): 26.

Knowles, Loraine. "The Career Position of Women in Museums." *Museums Journal* 88 (September 1988): 61–65.

Legget, Jane A. 1984. "Women in Museums—Past, Present and Future." In *Women, Heritage, and Museums Conference Proceedings.* Manchester: Social History Curators Group.

Lerner, Gerda. *The Majority Finds Its Past: Placing Women in History.* New York: Oxford University Press, 1979.

Mainardi, Patricia. "Museums and Revisionism." *Australian Journal of Art* 7 (1988): 4–15.

Mark, Joan. "Alice C. Fletcher." In *Four Anthropologists: An American Science in its Early Years.* New York: Science History Publications, 1980.

Marshall, Anne. "Employment in the Eyes of the Law." *Museum News* 51 (March 1973): 27–39.

Matsushita, Tomoko. "In Japan: The Volunteers of the National Science Museum." *Museum* 171 (1991): 144.

Mayo, Edith P. "A New View?" *Museum News* 69 (July-August 1990): 48–50.

Melosh, Barbara, and Christina Simmons. "Exhibiting Women's History." In *Presenting the Past: Essays on History and the Public,* eds. Susan Porter Benson, Stephen Brier, and Roy Rosenzweig, 203–21. Philadelphia: Temple University Press, 1986.

Museum 171 (1991). Special issue, "Focus on Women."

Museum News 69 (July-August 1990). Four-article anthology, "Making a Difference: Women in Museums."

Museums Journal 88 (September 1988). Special issue on women and museums.

National Commission on the Observance of International Women's Year. *The Creative Woman: A Report of the Committee on the Arts and Humanities.* Washington, D.C., 1975.

Nemser, Cindy. "Art Criticism and Gender Prejudice." *Arts Magazine* 46 (March 1972): 44–46.

Nilson, Lisbet. "Coming of Age." *Artnews* 87 (October 1988): 104–9.

Nochlin, Linda. "Why Have There Been No Great Women Artists?" *Artnews* 69 (January 1971): 22–39, 67–71. (Reprinted in Nochlin, Linda. *Women, Art, and Power and Other Essays.* New York: Harper and Row, 1988.)

Pantykina, Irina. "USSR: Three Portraits." *Museum* 171 (1991): 155–57.

"Pioneers in American Museums: Agnes Mongan." *Museum News* 54 (September-October 1975): 30–33.

Pollock, Griselda. *Vision and Difference: Femininity, Feminism, and Histories of Art.* London: Routledge, 1988.

Porter, Gaby. "Are You Sitting Comfortably?" *Museums Journal* 90 (November 1990): 25–27.

———. 1986. "Gender Bias: Representations of Work in History Museums." Proceedings of the Annual Study Weekend, "Bias in Museums," ed. Annette Carruthers. In *Museum Professionals Group Transactions* 22 (1986): 11–15. Exeter, England, 1986.

———. "How Are Women Represented in British History Museums?" *Museum* 171 (1991): 159–62.

———. "Putting Your House in Order: Representations of Women and Domestic Life." In *The Museum Time-Machine: Putting Cultures on Display,* ed. Robert Lumley, 102–27. London: Routledge, 1988.

Prince, David R. "Women in Museums." *Museums Journal* 88 (September 1988): 55–60.

Ray, Amita. "India: New Paths in the Shifting Sand." *Museum* 171 (1991): 152–54.

Richardson, Brenda. "Berkeley and the Women's Movement." *Museum News* 51 (March 1973): 40–44.

Robertson, Nan. *The Girls in the Balcony: Women, Men, and the New York Times.* New York: First Ballentine Books, 1993.

Rosen, Randy, and Catherine C. Brawer. *Making Their Mark: Women Artists Move into the Mainstream, 1970–85.* Exhibition catalog. New York: Abbeville Press, 1989.

Rosser, Sue V. "Feminist Scholarship in the Sciences: Where Are We Now and Where Can We Expect a Theoretical Breakthrough?" In *Feminism and Science,* ed. Nancy Tuana. Bloomington: Indiana University Press, 1989.

———, ed. *Feminism within the Science and Health Care Professions: Overcoming Resistance.* Oxford and New York: Pergamon Press, 1988.

Rossiter, Margaret W. *Women Scientists in America: Struggles and Strategies to 1940.* Baltimore: Johns Hopkins University Press, 1982.

Rozsika, Parker, and Griselda Pollock, eds. *Framing Feminism: Art and the Women's Movement 1970–85.* London: Routledge and Kegan Paul, 1987.

Scott, Joan Wallach. *Gender and the Politics of History.* New York: Columbia University Press, 1988.

Sellers, Jane. "Managing Museums with Women in Mind." *Feminist Arts News* 3 (1991): 6.

Shaman, Sanford Sivitz. "Planning for 'The Responsible Stimulation of Ideas and Opinions.'" *International Journal of Museum Management and Curatorship* 6 (September 1987): 271–76.

Sherman, Claire Richter, and Adele M. Holcomb, eds. *Women as Interpreters of the Visual Arts, 1820–1979.* Westport, Conn.: Greenwood Press, 1981.

Showalter, Elaine, ed. *The New Feminist Criticism: Essays on Women, Literature, and Theory.* New York: Pantheon Books, 1985.

Smith, Barbara Clark, and Kathy Peiss. *Men and Women: A History of Costume, Gender, and Power.* Washington, D.C.: National Museum of American History, 1989.

Steinem, Gloria. *Revolution from Within.* Boston: Little Brown, 1991.

Stitt, Susan. *The Museum Labor Market: A Survey of American Historical Agency Placement Opportunities, Part I.* Sturbridge, Mass.: Old Sturbridge Village, 1976.

———. "The Search for Equality." *Museum News* 54 (September-October 1975): 17–23.

Taylor, Kendall. "Risking It: Women as Museum Leaders." *Museum News* 63 (February 1985): 20–32.

———. "To Create Credibility." *Museum News* 69 (July-August 1990): 41–42.

Thomas, David Hurst. "Margaret Mead as a Museum Anthropologist." *American Anthropologist* 82 (June 1980): 354–61.

Trucco, Terry. "Where Are the Women Museum Directors?" *Artnews* 76 (February 1977): 52–57.

Tuana, Nancy, ed. *Feminism and Science.* Bloomington: Indiana University Press, 1989.

Tucker, Marcia. "Common Ground." *Museum News* 69 (July-August 1990): 44–46.

Tuminaro, Dominick, and Ashton Hawkins. "You've Come a Long Way . . . " *Museum News* 50 (June 1972): 27–35.

Ullberg, Patricia, and Joanna H. Wos. "The Right Preparation and the Right Attitude." *Museum News* 63 (February 1985): 33–36.

Wallace, Michael. "The Future of History Museums." *History News* 44 (July-August 1989): 5–8, 30–33.

———. "Reflections on the History of Historic Preservation." In *Presenting the Past: Essays on History and the Public,* eds. Susan Porter Benson, Stephen Brier, and Roy Rosenzweig, 165–99. Philadelphia: Temple University Press, 1986.

Wilkinson, S., et al. "Soldiering On." *Museums Journal* 91 (November 1991): 22–28.

Women's Changing Roles in Museums. 1986. Conference Proceedings, ed. Ellen Cochran Hicks. Washington, D.C.: Office of Museum Programs, Smithsonian Institution and Smithsonian Institution Women's Council.

Zelevansky, Lynn. "Interview with Linda Shearer." *Women Artists News* 13 (Fall 1988): 17–18.

Compiled by Maureen Grove Turman

Contributors

JOALLYN ARCHAMBAULT, Director of American Indian Programs, National Museum of Natural History, Smithsonian Institution, Washington, D.C.

MALCOLM ARTH, former Director of Education, American Museum of Natural History, New York (now deceased).

ESIN ATIL, Historian of Islamic Art, Freer Gallery of Art and Arthur M. Sackler Gallery, Smithsonian Institution, Washington, D.C.

LOIS W. BANNER, Professor of History, University of Southern California, Los Angeles.

CLAUDINE BROWN, Deputy Assistant Secretary for Arts and Humanities, Smithsonian Institution, Washington, D.C.

MARY SCHMIDT CAMPBELL, Dean, Tisch School of the Arts, New York University, New York.

TOM CROUCH, Chairperson, Department of Aeronautics, National Air and Space Museum, Smithsonian Institution, Washington, D.C.

E. KAY DAVIS, Executive Director, Fernbank Museum of Natural History, Atlanta.

LINDA DOWNS, Head of Education, Department of Education, National Gallery of Art, Washington, D.C.

ZORA MARTIN FELTON, Chief, Department of Education, Anacostia Museum, Smithsonian Institution, Washington, D.C.

VICTORIA FUNK, Curator, Department of Botany, National Museum of Natural History, Smithsonian Institution, Washington, D.C.

JANE R. GLASER, Special Assistant, Office of the Assistant Secretary for Arts and Humanities, Smithsonian Institution, Washington, D.C.

MARGERY GORDON, Education Specialist, Office of Education, National Museum of Natural History, Smithsonian Institution, Washington, D.C.

ANN W. LEWIN, President, National Learning Center and Capital Children's Museum, Washington, D.C.

ROGER MANDLE, President, Rhode Island School of Design, Providence.

EDITH P. MAYO, Curator, Division of Political History, Department of Social and Cultural History, National Museum of American History, Smithsonian Institution, Washington, D.C.

LILLIAN B. MILLER, Historian of American Culture and Editor of the Charles Willson Peale Papers, National Portrait Gallery, Smithsonian Institution, Washington, D.C.

CHRISTINA ORR-CAHALL, Director, Norton Gallery and School of Art, West Palm Beach, Florida.

MARC PACHTER, Deputy Assistant Secretary for External Affairs, Smithsonian Institution, Washington, D.C.

HEATHER PAUL, Vice President of Planning, National Health Council, Washington, D.C.

PAUL N. PERROT, Director, Santa Barbara Museum of Art, Santa Barbara, California.

PHILIP RAVENHILL, Chief Curator, National Museum of African Art, Smithsonian Institution, Washington, D.C.

BARBARA CLARK SMITH, Curator, Division of Domestic Life, Department of Social and Cultural History, National Museum of American History, Smithsonian Institution, Washington, D.C.

JANET W. SOLINGER, former Director of the Resident Associates Program, Smithsonian Institution, Washington, D.C.

KATHY DWYER SOUTHERN, Director, National Cultural Alliance, Washington, D.C.

ROWENA STEWART, Executive Director, Motown Historical Museum, Detroit.

SUSAN STITT, President, Historical Society of Pennsylvania, Philadelphia.

ROBERT SULLIVAN, Associate Director of Public Programs, National Museum of Natural History, Smithsonian Institution, Washington, D.C.

FRANK TALBOT, former Director, National Museum of Natural History, Smithsonian Institution, Washington, D.C.

KENDALL TAYLOR, Academic Director, Museum Studies and the Arts Program, Washington Semester, American University, Washington, D.C.

MARCIA TUCKER, Director, The New Museum of Contemporary Art, New York.

MAUREEN GROVE TURMAN, Assistant to the Deputy Director, Hirshhorn Museum and Sculpture Garden, Smithsonian Institution, Washington, D.C.

BONNIE VANDORN, Director, Association of Science and Technology Centers, Washington, D.C.

JEAN WEBER, Director, Maine Maritime Museum, Augusta.

ARTEMIS A. ZENETOU, Program Coordinator and Editor, Office of the Assistant Secretary for Arts and Humanities, Smithsonian Institution, Washington, D.C.